REPENTANCE

THE MOST MISUNDERSTOOD WORD IN THE BIBLE

REPENTANCE

THE MOST MISUNDERSTOOD WORD IN THE BIBLE

G. Michael Cocoris

Grace Gospel Press
Milwaukee, Wisconsin

G. Michael Cocoris
2016 Euclid #20, Santa Monica, CA 90405
(310) 396-3132
email: michael@cocoris.com
website: www.insightsfromtheword.com

ISBN: 978-0-9799637-7-3

Library of Congress Control Number: 2010929785

Grace Gospel Press
10328 W. Oklahoma Ave.
Milwaukee, WI 53227
U.S.A.
www.gracegospelpress.com

Contents

PREFACE

When I was converted at age eighteen, I realized that I was a sinner and that Christ died in my place to pay for my sins. I was overwhelmed that God loved a sinner such as I. I trusted Jesus Christ. I wept. My life was transformed.

Soon after my conversion I heard preachers saying that in order to be saved one must repent, insisting that repentance is a change in lifestyle. They said things like, "You must turn from your sins." I didn't know much Bible or theology, but it seemed to me that what they were saying was incompatible with the gospel of the grace of God. In some cases it sounded to me like the preacher was telling people they had to change their life before they could come to Christ to be changed by Him!

About that time, someone told me that the word "repent" meant a "change of mind." That satisfied me, but, frankly, I still wondered about some passages of Scripture.

Years later, I decided to do a study of repentance. I looked up every occurrence of the words "repent" and "repentance" in the New Testament, only to discover that in most cases those words did not have an object. The content of repentance had to be determined from the context. I chose to limit my conclusions primarily to those instances in which the word repent was followed by an object. For example, "repentance from dead works" in Hebrews 6:1 clearly indicates that the object of repentance is dead works. Also, I concluded that, although the word "repent" in Acts 2:38 does not have an object, the evidence from the context is overwhelming that Peter is speaking about repentance concerning Jesus Christ. Based on that study I decided that there are four objects of repentance, namely God, Christ, dead works, and sin. That is what I put in my book *Evangelism: A Biblical Approach* (1984).

In 1985, Robert Wilkin submitted his doctoral dissertation entitled, "Repentance as a Condition for Salvation in the New Testament" to Dallas Theological Seminary. Sometime after that, I received a copy, read it, and filed it. Many years later (2003), I decided to revisit the subject of repentance. In the process I reread Wilkin's dissertation. I mention Wilkin's dissertation here because I found it very helpful, but since Wilkin wrote his dissertation, he has changed his view of repentance. A revised version of his dissertation was published in a series of six articles in the *Journal of the Grace Evangelical Society* and so was an article explaining his change of mind. (See bibliography for details; all articles can be seen at www.faithalone.org.) I refer to both his dissertation and his six articles.

When a person's name appears alone in parentheses, it is the name of a commentator, who is commenting on the verse under consideration. The name of the commentary, etc. is in the bibliography. All other references in the text will give the title of the book and the page number. I also wish to thank Teresa Roger for proofreading this material.

Repentance is an important subject. It is required for salvation. Unfortunately, it is one of the most abused subjects in the New Testament. May the Lord be pleased to use this study to clarify the meaning of repentance so that we proclaim a clear message concerning what God has said people must do in order to receive the gift of eternal life.

G. Michael Cocoris
Santa Monica, CA

Chapter 1

THE PROBLEMS WITH REPENTANCE

Repentance is one of the most important words in the Bible. Jesus commissions it to be preached "to all nations" (Lk. 24:47). God commands "all men everywhere to repent" (Acts 17:30). He desires that "all should come to repentance" (2 Pet. 3:9). Repentance is important because repentance is necessary for salvation. Chafer wrote, "Therefore, it is as dogmatically stated as language can declare, that repentance is essential to salvation and that none could be saved, apart from repentance" (Chafer, vol. 3, p. 373).

Repentance is the most misunderstood word in the Bible. What most think is repentance is not repentance at all. What is often said to be repentance may be related to repentance, coming before it, or resulting from it, but is not the *nature* of repentance. The definition of repentance is definitely a difficulty and so is the relationship of repentance to faith. Is repentance separate from, or inseparable from, faith?

These are critical issues because repentance is such an important subject. Since repentance is so important and since it is so misunderstood, it is imperative that it be carefully examined to determine exactly what the Biblical message of repentance is. First, the problems connected with repentance need to be clarified.

Definition of Repent

Change Your Mind

Some say that the word "repent" simply means "To change your mind." Chafer says, "The word (repentance) means *a change of mind*" (Chafer, vol. 3, p. 372). Ryrie states, "In both the Old and New Testaments repentance means 'to change one's mind'" (Ryrie, *So Great Salvation*, hereafter *SGS*, p. 92). Baker writes, "It (repentance) refers to reconsidering or changing the mind after an action has taken place" (Baker, p. 411). Others have also concluded that repentance means a change of mind.

Be Sorry for Sin

It is commonly assumed that repentance is being sorry for sin. Webster defines the religious usage of "repent" as "to feel so contrite over one's sins as to change, or decide to change, one's way; be penitent." Barclay says, "Repentance is the admission that the fault is ours and the experience of godly sorrow that it is so" (Barclay, *The Revelation of John*, vol. 1, p. 79).

Be Willing to Stop Sinning

According to this view, repentance is not actually turning from sin; it is a *decision* to do so. Erickson declares, "It is important for us to understand the nature of true repentance. Repentance is godly sorrow for one's sin together with a resolution to turn from it" (Erickson, p. 937).

Turning from Sin

Berkhof defines repentance as "change wrought in the conscious life of the sinner, by which he turns away from sin" (Berkhof, p. 486). Another says, "To repent means literally to change direction, and in the New Testament it means to change the direction of one's life. To repent means that one has been (negatively) headed down the wrong path, but now (positively) shifts to the right path" (Hanson, p. 242). Repentance is said to be the "forsaking of sin, and turning from it" (Barnes on Rom. 2:4).

Acts of Penance

Early in church history, the idea arose that original sin and all sins prior to baptism were removed by baptism. As a result, people waited until they were near death before they got baptized. To deal with that problem, it was taught that repentance was the cure for post-baptismal sins. Repentance was said to consist of feeling sorry for and confessing post-baptismal sins, as well as doing acts of penance. The Greek words "repent" and "repentance" were translated into Latin by words that meant "do acts of penance" and "acts of penance" (Wilkin, *JOTGES*, Autumn, 1988, pp. 12-13).

When Jerome (ca. 340-420 A.D.) produced the Latin Vulgate Bible, he retained the Old Latin practice of translating "repent" as "do acts of repentance." John Wycliffe (ca. 1320-1384), who was the first to translate the Bible into English, did not base his translation on the original Hebrew and Greek, but on the Latin Vulgate. Following the Latin Vulgate, he translated "repentance" as "do penance." When the Roman Catholic Douay version was produced (1609-1610) it did the same (Wilkin, Autumn 1989, pp. 16-17). Thus, the Roman Catholic view of repentance is that it consists of contrition, confession, and performing acts of penance.

Relationship to Faith

Faith Alone

The Bible is emphatic that salvation is by faith. Moses wrote that Abraham "believed in the Lord, and He accounted it to him for righteousness" (Gen. 15:6). Jesus said, "For God so loved the world that He gave His only begotten Son, that whoever believes in Him should not perish but have everlasting life" (Jn. 3:16). Paul proclaimed, "Believe on the Lord Jesus Christ, and you will be saved" (Acts 16:31). In these and many other passages, faith is the one and only requirement for salvation.

Not only does the Bible repeatedly mention faith as the single requirement, but also in critical places it does not mention repentance. The Gospel of John is the only book in the Bible that has as its purpose to bring people to Christ. At the end of his Gospel, John wrote, "And truly Jesus did many other signs in the presence of His disciples, which are not written in this book, but these are written that you may believe that Jesus is the Christ, the Son of God, and that believing you may have life in His name" (Jn. 20:31). Yet the Gospel of John does not mention the words "repent" or "repentance" one single time.

The most detailed book in the Bible on salvation is the book of Romans. The chapter in Romans on what one must do to be saved is Romans 4, but Romans 4 does not contain the words "repent" or "repentance." In fact, the word "repentance" only occurs once in the book of Romans (Rom. 2:4) and there it is a virtual synonym for faith.

The only book in the Bible written to defend the Gospel is Galatians. Neither the word "repent" nor the word "repentance" makes an appearance in that book at all.

Repentance Alone

On the other hand, some passages say that repentance is required (Lk. 24:47; Acts 2:38; 3:19; 5:31; 17:30; 26:20; 2 Pet. 3:9; Rev. 9:20-21; 16:9, 11) and in these verses there is no mention of faith!

Faith and Repentance Together

To complicate matters, faith and repentance appear together in three places (Mk. 1:16; Acts 20:21; Heb. 6:1). The absence of repentance in critical passages on salvation and yet the insistence on repentance in others is a problem. What is the relationship between faith and repentance?

Summary: The problems with repentance are its definition and its relationship to faith. In order to sort all of this out, it is necessary to do word studies of the words "repent" and "repentance" and examine every occurrence of these words in the New Testament.

Chapter 2

THE MEANING OF REPENTANCE

3rd Century def.

One popular conception is that "repent" means "to be sorry for sin." Preachers often proclaim that it means "to turn from sin." In both of these definitions repentance has to do with sin. While not all professors agree, some say it means "to change one's mind" and that it does not necessarily have to do with sin. Who is right? It is obvious that some of these definitions are wrong, because they mutually exclude each other. It cannot be that repentance is always about sin and that it is not necessarily about sin at all.

1st cent Def

Then, there is that problem of the relationship between faith and repentance. Why is it that faith usually occurs alone without any mention of repentance, but sometimes repentance is used without any mention of faith? *Synech*

Definition

What the Definition Is

How is the definition of a word determined? Most people simply look words up in a dictionary and accept what it says, but how does a dictionary determine the meanings of words? Compilers of a dictionary determine the meaning of a word by its *usage*. Based on all the ways a word is being used, dictionaries list all its *possible* meanings, called "the field of meaning." The meaning of a word is determined by its usage at a given time in a given context.

In the following chapters each of the fifty-eight occurrences of "repent" and "repentance" in the New Testament will be examined. It will be demonstrated that in the New Testament these words mean "a change of mind." Many passages contain indications in the context that repentance is a change of mind.

For example, in Acts 8, Peter and John laid hands on believers in Samaria for them to receive the Holy Spirit (Acts 8:14-17). When Simon saw what they were doing, he offered them money for the power to do it himself (Acts 8:18-19). In no uncertain terms, Peter told Simon to repent (Acts 8:22). From the context of the conversation, it is clear Simon had not done anything wrong in the sense of some external act, such as murder, adultery, or stealing. Peter plainly said that Simon's problem was what he was thinking. Peter said, "Your money perish with you, because you *thought* that the gift of God could be purchased with money!" (Acts 8:20, italics added). Furthermore, Peter told Simon, "Your *heart* is not right in the sight of God" (Acts 8:21, italics added) and "Pray God if perhaps the *thought of your heart* may be forgiven you" (Acts 8:22. italics added). It is unmistakable that in Acts 8, "repent" is an internal change in thinking.

Granted, the meaning of a word is determined by its usage and this is only one passage. Repent could have a different meaning in another passage. The term "trunk" can mean "the main stem of a tree, the torso of a human body, a large box used for storage, a compartment of a car, and the nose of an elephant," depending on the context. That is why every appearance of the words "repent" and repentance" must be examined in context. For the technical method of doing a word study, see Appendix 1.

There are Greek authorities who say that the meaning of the Greek word for "repent" in the New Testament is "to change one's mind." For example, one Greek lexicon says that the Greek word translated "repent" means "to change one's mind or purpose" and "repentance," means "after-thought" (Abbott-Smith). In his comments on Matthew 3:2, A. T. Robertson, the great Greek scholar, defines "repent" as a "change (think afterwards) [of] their mental attitudes" (see his *Word Pictures in the New Testament*). Julius R. Mantey, who co-authored the famous *A Manual Grammar of the Greek New Testament* (known as "Dana and Mantey") says, "It means to think differently or have

[handwritten: Manley is wrong — the change of mind is from any other means of salv'to to Christ alone for salv.]

a different attitude toward sin and God, etc." (Mantey, *Basic Christian Doctrine*, p. 193).

There are theologians who concur. Chafer says, "The word (repentance) means a change of mind" (Chafer, vol. 3, p. 372). Even Erickson, who pours more into the word, admits that "literally" it means, "to think differently about something or have a change of mind" (Erickson, p. 937). Ryrie defines the word "repent" as "to change your mind" (Ryrie, *SBD*, p. 139).

There are commentators who agree. In his comments on Luke 3:3, Alfred Plummer calls repentance "an inward change of mind." In his commentary on Hebrews 6:1, Bishop Westcott says, "It follows, therefore, that 'Repentance *from* dead works' expresses the complete change of mind—of spiritual attitude—which leads the believer to abandon these works and seek some other support for life."

Simply put the Greek words for "repent" and "repentance" describe an inward change of thinking or attitude.

A Clarification

It is commonly assumed that repentance always concerns sin. That is not the case. The Greek words rendered "repent" and "repentance" mean "a change of mind or attitude"—period. What people change their mind about is not in, or implied by, the word repent. The issue may be sin or it may not be. It is used of sin and it is used of repenting of something good! "Plutarch tells of two murderers, who having spared a child, afterwards 'repented' and sought to slay it" (Trench, p. 258).

The Greek word "repentance" is like the English "dozen." The word "dozen" means "twelve." It does not contain or imply twelve of one particular thing; it simply means "twelve." A farmer might use the word "dozen" referring to eggs, while a baker may use it in reference to donuts. Does "dozen" mean twelve *eggs* or twelve *donuts*? The answer is neither. It simply means, "twelve"—period. The context (the farm or the bakery) determines its object. R. A. Torrey said, "What the repentance, or change of mind, is about must always be determined by the context" (Torrey, p. 355).

What the Definition Is Not

Admittedly, not all agree that repentance is simply a change of mind. As was noted in the previous chapter, some define repentance as being sorry and/or turning from sin. One Greek lexicon says "repent" means to "change one's mind" and later states, that it means "feel remorse, repent, be converted" and "repentance" means "change of mind, remorse, turning away, a turning about" (Arndt and Gingrich).

Those who claim that repentance means, "to feel remorse" begin with what they say is one of the Old Testament words for repentance. For a word study of the Hebrew word "sorrow," see Appendix 2. Besides, the actual use, not one possible meaning out of a field of meanings, determines the meaning of a word. The issue, the only issue, is how the word "repent" is used in the New Testament.

In the New Testament, repentance is definitely *not* being sorry for sin. It makes a distinction between remorse and repentance. There is another Greek word for regret (*metamelomai*). It appears five times in the New Testament (Mt. 21:29, 32; 27:3; 2 Cor. 7:8; Heb. 7:21). This word describes "sorrow for something done and wishing it undone," but "forgiveness of sins is nowhere promised" for it (Trench, p. 258). Judas was "remorseful" (Mt. 27:3), but he did not get saved. On the other hand, the Greek word for repentance (*metanoia*) "does not properly signify sorrow for having done amiss" (Trench, p. 257). Esau shed tears, but it did change anything (Heb. 12:16-17).

Paul plainly demonstrates that sorrow and repentance are two different things. He says, "Your sorrow led to repentance" (2 Cor. 7:9). Sorrow may lead to repentance; sorrow may accompany repentance, but sorrow and repentance are two different things.

The New Testament records an illustration of the difference between regretting and repenting. In Acts 2, the Jews regretted what they did to Christ. They were "cut to the heart" and asked, "What shall we do?" (Acts 2:37). It was *after their regret* that Peter said, "Repent" (Acts 2:38), which shows that regret is different than repentance.

It should be pointed out that sorrow does not have to precede repentance. Paul says the goodness of God can also lead to repentance (Rom. 2:4). D. L. Moody used to say the inquirer is not to seek for sorrow, but for the Savior. Gill says, "Tears of repentance will not wash away sin; notwithstanding these, iniquity remains marked before God; Christ's tears themselves did not take away, nor atone for sin; His blood must be shed, and it was shed for the remission of it; and that is the only meritorious cause of it" (Gill on Lk. 24:47).

When some change their minds, there may be emotions—and there may not be. When people change their mind, a change of action is expected, but both of these things are *results* of repentance, and not the nature of repentance. "Nowhere is man exhorted to feel a certain amount of sorrow for his sins in order to come to Christ" (Ironside, p. 12). *Not "Results"*

This Border on area - Bad idea

Those who say that repentance means "Turn from sin" claim that one of the Hebrew words for "repentance" means "to turn." For a word study of the Hebrew word "turn," see Appendix 3. Besides, the meaning of any word is determined by usage. So the question is, "Does the term 'repent' mean 'turn' in the New Treatment?"

In the New Testament, repentance is definitely *not* turning from sin. It makes a distinction between repentance and turning. There is another Greek word for turning (*epistrephō*) and it is never translated "to repent" (Wilkin, dissertation, p. 11). Acts 26:20 clearly demonstrates that repenting and turning are two different things. Paul says that the Gentiles should "repent *and* turn to God" (literal translation).

Furthermore, the New Testament speaks about repenting *and* bringing forth fruit fit for repentance (Lk. 3:8; Acts 26:20), which indicates that repenting is different than turning from sin. In his commentary on Luke 3:8, Lenski states, "Repentance cannot be meant by 'fruits' . . . 'Fruits' indicate an organic connection between themselves and repentance just as the tree brings the fruit that is particular to its nature . . . [Repentance] is invisible; hence, we judge its presence by the [fruits], which are visible." Berkhof points out that the Roman Catholic Church "externalized the idea of repentance entirely" (Berkhof, p. 486) and adds, "Over against this external view of repentance the Scriptural idea should be maintained. According to Scripture, repentance is wholly an inward act, and should not be confounded with the change of life that (proceeds) from it. Confession of sin and reparation of wrongs are *fruits* of repentance" (Berkhof, p. 487).

Can proceed

Luke 17:1-4 is an illustration that proves the point. Jesus teaches that if a man repents seven times in one day, he is to be forgiven seven times. There is no question that there is genuine repentance here—the whole point assumes that the repentance is genuine. Yet this genuine repentance did not affect the man's lifestyle!

So, repentance is not being sorry for sin or turning from sin. The way that some get sorry for sin or turning from sin out of repentance is by claiming that New Testament repentance is based on the Old Testament, but there is no technical term for repentance in the Old Testament. So, some say that while the word is not there, the "concept" is there (Kittel, vol. 4, p. 980). Then they go to the Hebrew words for sorrow or turn, but, as the studies in the Appendices demonstrate, the connection is not valid. Those using this approach are *assuming* that repentance is feeling sorrow for sin or turning from sin. Then, they find words that have those definitions. Their boat does not float on a sea of facts.

The conclusive evidence that repentance does not mean to be sorry for sin or to turn from sin is that in the Old Testament, *God* repents! To illustrate, in the King James Version of the Old Testament, the word *repent* occurs forty-six times. Thirty-seven of these times, God is the one repenting (or not repenting). If repentance means sorrow for sin or turning from sin, God would be a sinner.

Relationship to Faith

The word "repent" is used in passages pertaining to salvation and in passages that do not concern salvation. What is the relationship between faith and repentance in salvation? Several possible solutions have been suggested.

Not a Requirement

Hodges is not exactly clear as to his definition of repentance. In a footnote, he explains that the concept of "sorrow" or "remorse" is "frequently implied," but "by no means always implied" (Hodges, *AS*, p. 224). Since "remorse" is not always present, he seems to conclude that the meaning is "regret" (Hodge, *AS*, p. 224). Be that as it may, Hodges is clear that in his opinion repentance "is not essential to the saving transaction as such, it is in no sense a condition for that transaction" (Hodges, *AS*, p. 146). It is "not a condition for eternal life" (Hodges, *AS*, p. 158). Repentance is the condition for fellowship with God (Hodges, *AS*, p. 146). It is "the call to enter into harmonious relations with God" (Hodges, *AS*, p. 145).

The problem with this proposal is that in some passages, repentance is given as the sole requirement of salvation (Lk. 24:47; Acts 17:30; 2 Pet. 3:9).

Required, but a Separate Step

One possible solution is that repentance and faith are two separate "steps" to salvation. Erickson calls repentance a "prerequisite for salvation" (Erickson, p. 937). If it is a necessary, separate step, why is it not mentioned in the Gospel of John, in Romans 4 and the book of Galatians?

Required and Inseparable

Many passages indicate that when it comes to salvation, faith and repentance are inseparably linked together. To the people assembled in Cornelius' house, Peter preached, "Whoever believes in Him (Jesus) will receive remission of sins" (Acts 10:43). No mention is made of repentance. In fact, the word does not occur in Acts 10—at all, not even once! Yet when Peter reported to the apostles and brethren in Jerusalem what happened, they said, "God has also granted to the Gentiles repentance to life" (Acts 11:18).

John Calvin says, "Can true repentance exist without faith? By no means. But although they cannot be separated, they ought to be distinguished" (Calvin, *Institutes*, 3, 3, 5). Many have followed Calvin. For example, Berkhof states, "True repentance never exists except in conjunction with faith, while, on the other hand, wherever there is true faith, there is also real repentance. . . . The two cannot be separated; they are simply complementary parts of the same process" (Berkhof, p. 487). Erickson agrees, "As we examine repentance and faith, it should be remembered that they cannot really be separated from one another" (Erickson, p. 935). In a sermon entitled "Faith and Repentance Inseparable" Charles Haddon Spurgeon put it like this: "The repentance which is here commanded is the result of faith;

No—it results in faith.

[handwritten top: Simple ∴ One believes because he HAS changed his mind from old system of salv. to faith in XP for salv. wrong]

it is <u>born at the same time with faith</u>—they are twins, and to say which is the elder-born passes my knowledge. It is a great mystery; faith is <u>before repentance in some of its acts</u>, and repentance before faith in another view of it; the fact being that they come into the soul together."

[handwritten: No !!! One cannot have faith w/o having changed its mind to come to that faith.]

Summary: Repentance, which means a change of mind or attitude, not tears or turning from sin, is inseparable from faith in salvation.

[handwritten: Not inseparable—for one can repent in non-salvific issues]

To define repentance as being sorry for sin or turning from sin is dangerous. It causes people to think they <u>can do something</u> that in some way would <u>help them obtain salvation</u>. For example, when salvation is made to be conditioned on feelings (being sorry), it encourages people "to look inward at themselves and not away to Christ as Savior." They are led "to measure the validity of their salvation by the intensity of anguish which preceded or accompanied it." In such a way "sorrow of heart becomes a most subtle form of meritorious work and to that extent a contradiction of grace" (Chafer, vol. 3, p. 373).

Calling the view that repentance is turning from sin "terribly dangerous," Wilkin says that instead of pointing people to Christ and the cross, <u>it points their attention to their own efforts at reformation</u> and it also "undermines assurance" (Wilkin, *JOTGES*, Spring, 1991, p. 17). Preaching that people must turn from their sin can cause genuinely saved people, especially perfectionists, to begin doubting the reality of their salvation, because in their opinion, they did not have enough tears or turning away from sinful habits at the time they trusted Christ. Thus, preaching repentance as turning from sin is not only unbiblical, it undermines assurance.

Repentance is a change of mind—period. A change of mind *[handwritten: No / May —]* should result in a change in behavior, but the word *repent* looks at the change of belief, not the change in behavior. Repentance is the root; change in behavior is the fruit.

My wife, Patricia, who is a talented interpreter for the deaf (she interrupted in a public High school for eleven and a half years and in the court system for many years), tells me that in sign language, the sign for "repent" is made up of two signs (it's a compound word!), one for "change" and another for "mind." There are other signs for changing your actions or behavior.

[handwritten: Good]

Interesting. The deaf, who can't hear, have it right. Maybe, some do not have it right because of what they have "heard." Perhaps, they should *look* at what is said in the Word instead of *listening* to what others say.

Repent/a change of mind is inherent to new faith for new salvation. One cannot believe in something for the 1st time w/o a change of mind before hand.

Chapter 3

THE MESSAGE OF JOHN THE BAPTIST

Context

Because the meaning of a word is determined by its usage, to determine the meaning of the words "repent" and "repentance" in the New Testament, each occurrence of these words in the New Testament should be carefully examined. The Greek words for "repent" and "repentance" occur fifty-eight times in the New Testament. (The verb appears 34 times and the noun 24.) Some of these references refer to the same occasion (for example, Mt. 11:21 and Lk. 10:13) or to the same thing (Mt. 3:11; Mk. 1:4; Lk. 3:3; Acts 13:24; 19:4). Therefore, the New Testament mentions repentance about 41 separate times.

John the Baptist was the first person in the New Testament to preach repentance. Eight of the 58 occurrences of repent and repentance refer to his ministry. He preached "repent" (Mt. 3:2) and he practiced a baptism of repentance (Mt. 3:11; Mk. 1:4; Lk. 3:3; Acts 13:24; 19:4). He also proclaimed that those who did repent should bring forth fruit fitting the repentance (Mt. 3:8; Lk. 3:8).

John's Message

Change Your Mind

John the Baptist preached, "Repent, for the kingdom of heaven is at hand!" (Mt. 3:2). Several clues in this passage indicate that by "repent" John meant a change of mind. In Matthew 3:9, John says, "Do not *think* (italics added) to say to yourself, 'We have

Abraham as our father.'" (According to Luke, John said, "Do not begin to say to yourselves;" see Lk. 3:8.)

The Jews of John's day were of the opinion that being a son of Abraham was a "pledge of safety" (M'Neile), that because they were the descendents of Abraham they had a part in the world to come (Edersheim; Barclay). Thus, John is telling people who thought that they would enter the kingdom because they were descendents of Abraham that they must "repent, for the kingdom of heaven is at hand." That is, they must not *think* that because they are descendents of Abraham they will enter the kingdom. Obviously, they must think something else, which John mentions later, but the point is that when John the Baptist said, "Repent," he meant "change your mind" about what you think it takes to enter the kingdom.

Another indication that by "repent" John meant a change of mind is that he says, "Bear fruits worthy of repentance" (Mt. 3:8). John distinguishes between repentance (an inward change of mind) and the fruit of repentance (an external change). Commenting on this verse, M'Neile, a Cambridge professor, who wrote a commentary on the Greek text of Matthew, says "repent" means "not merely penitential sorrow, but a change of *nous*" (*nous* means "mind"). Therefore, by "repent" John means a change of mind, not a change of behavior. The repentance is the root; the change in behavior is the fruit.

So, John is telling people that they must change their minds about thinking that their ancestry would get them into the kingdom. They thought they had merit before God; they needed to change their minds about that. To say the same thing another way, they were *trusting* their merit, their ancestry.

Trust Christ

John's message also includes that people were to trust Christ. Matthew records that he says, "I indeed baptize you with water unto repentance, but He who is coming after me is mightier than I, whose sandals I am not worthy to carry. He will baptize you with the Holy Spirit and fire" (Mt. 3:11). Paul's comment is, "John indeed baptized with a baptism of repentance, saying to the people that they should *believe* on Him who would come after him, that is, on Christ Jesus" (Acts 19:4, italics added). Concerning John the Baptist, the Gospel of John says, "There was a man sent from God, whose name *was* John. This man came for a witness, to bear witness of the Light, that all through him might *believe*" (Jn. 1:6-7, italics added). Commenting on this passage, Westcott, a Cambridge professor, who wrote a commentary on the Greek text of the Gospel of John, says, "The basis of his (John the Baptist) preaching was repentance—inner self-renunciation—the end was faith." John's message definitely included the need for trusting Jesus Christ.

If they had to change their minds *from* thinking that they had merit to enter the kingdom, what did they need to change their minds *to* in order to get into the coming kingdom? If they had to cease trusting their merit, what must they trust? Taking all the New Testament says about the ministry of John the Baptist into account the answer is, "They must cease to trust their own merits and trust the coming Messiah."

To sum up, to people who thought that because they were the descendents of Abraham they had a part in the world to come (Mt. 3:9), John the Baptist proclaimed "repent, for the kingdom of heaven is at hand" (Mt. 3:2), and believe on the one who is to come (Mt. 3:11; Acts 19:4; Jn. 1:7). In other words, for John the Baptist, "repent" meant change your mind about trusting your merit to get into the coming kingdom to trusting the Messiah. Notice that repentance and faith are linked together.

In his doctoral dissertation, Wilkin reached the conclusion that the message of repentance preached by John the Baptist was that people should "give up their old attitude, which was essentially a self-righteous one" and "adopt an attitude of humble recognition of their sinfulness and need of God's mercy and forgiveness" (Wilkin, dissertation, p. 98).

John's Baptism

[handwritten: John's Bapt was identification w/Kgdm not invitation to Salv.]

Matthew 3:11

Those who repented were baptized (Mt. 3:6). John says that this was a baptism "unto repentance" (Mt. 3:11). What is a baptism unto repentance? In the Greek text, the word translated "unto" (*eis*) can mean "in order to get" or it can mean "because of" (Dana and Mantey, p. 104). The people of Nineveh repented "at" (*eis*) the preaching of Jonah (Mt. 12:41). They did not repent in

[handwritten: Bapt aft Pent was ident w/ Cross]

order to get the preaching of Jonah, but *because* of his preaching. John's baptism was not in order to get repentance; they were baptized *because* they had repented.

Mark 1:4

Marks sums up John's ministry by saying, "John came baptizing in the wilderness and preaching a baptism of repentance for the remission of sins" (Mk. 1:4). As compared to Matthew's account, Mark adds the phrase "for the remission of sins." Is John saying that they have to be baptized in order to obtain the remission of sins? No!

The New Testament connects *repentance* to the remission of sins (Acts 3:19; 5:31; see comments on Lk. 24:47 and Acts 2:38). Those who repented (and had their sins forgiven) were baptized. That order is clearly seen in Matthew's account (cf. Mt. 3:3, 6, 11; see the previous paragraph). Therefore, it is repentance, not baptism, which is for the remission of sins (Wilkin, dissertation, pp. 41, 142). The baptism is an act of identification with those who have repented and are waiting for the Messiah.

Luke 3:3

Luke echoes Mark's summary. He says John the Baptist preached "a baptism of repentance for the remission of sins" (Lk. 3:3). It is the same expression that was used in Mark 1:4, which means the remission of sins is connected to repentance. Thus, those who repented received the remission of sins and they were baptized as an identification with those who had recognized their need of God's mercy and were waiting for the coming of the Messiah (Mt. 3:11). Acceptance of The Kgdm offer

Acts 13:24

In the synagogue at Antioch in Pisidia, Paul preached. The purpose of his sermon was to proclaim justification by faith (Acts 13:39). The content of his sermon was designed to accomplish that purpose. In the course of his sermon he said, "After John had first preached, before His coming, the baptism of repentance to all the people of Israel" (Acts 13:24). Paul does not explain the baptism of repentance. Since he does not bother to give any explanation, it is safe to assume that he uses the word "repentance" the same way that John did, namely, of a change of mind from trust in one's merit before God to trust in the Messiah. Baptism was the symbol of that change of mind.

If Paul had meant something other than what John did, he would have had to say so. Furthermore, whatever his understanding, it would have been consistent with justification by faith or he would not have mentioned it at all, since, in that case, it would have defeated his purpose.

Acts 19:4

At Ephesus, Paul asked some disciples who had been baptized by John the Baptist, "Did you receive the Holy Spirit when you believed?" (Acts 19:2). When they told Paul that they had not so much as heard whether there is a Holy Spirit, Paul told them, "John indeed baptized with a baptism of repentance, saying to the people that they should believe on Him who would come after him, that is, on Christ Jesus" (Acts 19:4).

As is the case with Paul's reference to the baptism of repentance by John the Baptist in Acts 13:24, there is insufficient information in this passage to define exactly what Paul's understanding of John's use of repentance was. Again, as in Acts 13:24, since Paul does not bother to give any explanation, it is safe to assume that he uses the expression "baptism of repentance" the same way that John did (see comments on Acts 13:24).

John's Fruit of Repentance

Matthew 3:8

To the religious leaders John said, "Therefore bear fruits worthy of repentance" (Mt. 3:8). This statement demonstrates that there is a difference between an internal change of attitude and an external change of action. The internal change is the root and the external change of action is the fruit. As M'Neile says, "The fruit is not the change of heart, but the acts which result from it."

What does the fruit that John had in mind look like? Matthew does not specifically record the answer to that question. There is, however, a clue in Matthew and a specific answer in Luke. Matthew says that when people were baptized by John, they were

Kgdm Related sins = New Jewish Views

"confessing their sins" (Mt. 3:6). The confession of sins was part of the fruit of repentance, not the repentance (Strong, p. 834).

Luke 3:8

Kgdm Related

According to Luke, when John told people to "bear fruits worthy of repentance" (Lk. 3:8) and they asked, "What shall we do then?" (Lk. 3:10), John replied, "He who has two tunics, let him give to him who has none; and he who has food, let him do likewise. Then tax collectors also came to be baptized, and said to him, 'Teacher, what shall we do?' And he said to them, 'Collect no more than what is appointed for you.' Likewise the soldiers asked him, saying, 'And what shall we do?' So he said to them, 'Do not intimidate anyone or accuse falsely, and be content with your wages'" (Lk. 3:11-14).

In response to John's preaching, they ask, "What shall we do?" meaning "what shall we do that is worthy of repentance?" John gave them a detailed list of what fruit looks like. Tax collectors should not collect more in taxes than is required. Soldiers should not misuse authority by intimating anyone or accusing anyone falsely and by being content with their wages. In other words, the fruit of repentance consists of sharing, being honest, and being content. Those who have trusted God's mercy should show mercy.

No, it required chg of mind about Kgdm.

But to enter gdm Salv was - required

Summary: The message of John the Baptist was "repent," that is, change your thinking from trusting your merit before God to trusting the Messiah for the remission of sins, be baptized as a indication of the remission of sins and bring forth external fruit fitting your internal change of thinking.

2 Repent involved

To people who thought that because they were the descendents of Abraham they had a part in the world to come (Mt. 3:9), John the Baptist proclaimed "Repent, for the kingdom of heaven is at hand" (Mt. 3:2), and believe on the one who is to come (Mt. 3:11; Acts 19:4; Jn. 1:7). In other words, change your mind about trusting your merit to get into the world to come and trust the Messiah.

Ironside put it like this: "Those who submitted to his (John the Baptist's) baptism were practically saying: "In this act I declare my change of mind, my new attitude toward myself, my sins, and my God. I own my unworthiness, and I cast myself upon the infinite mercy of God, looking to Him for deliverance, counting on Him to forgive my sins and graciously fit me for the reception of the King and a place in the Kingdom of the heavens" (Ironside, p. 30). Ironside added, repentance is "the confession that one is utterly without merit, and if he is ever saved at all it can only be through the merits of our Lord Jesus Christ" (Ironside, p. 36). When Bernard of Clairvaux was dying, monks spoke to him of his merits. His response was, "Holy Jesus, Thy wounds are my merits" (Ironside, p. 44).

Chapter 4

THE MESSAGE OF JESUS

In 1896, a pastor wrote a novel. One hundred years later, in 1996, experts ranked it as the tenth-most-read book in the world. The pastor was Charles Sheldon and the book was *In His Steps*. The story is simple. A tramp challenged a church to live up to what they believed. When the tramp dies the pastor and the people in his church pledged to live their lives for one year asking themselves, "What would Jesus do?" More recently a group opposed to gas guzzling SUV's published an ad which asked, "What Would Jesus Drive?" A Christian doctor has written a book entitled, *What would Jesus Eat*?

I have often wanted to know, "What would Jesus say about a particular subject?" That is an excellent question to ask concerning the subject of repentance. We have looked at what John the Baptist meant by the word, but what would Jesus say?

Of the 58 times the words "repent" and "repentance" occur in the New Testament, 20 of them are used about the ministry of Jesus in the synoptic gospels. This includes the fact that He sent the disciples to preach repentance, which will be discussed in the next chapter, and that in the story He told about the rich man and Lazarus, it is the rich man who says something about repentance. Those 20 occurrences do not include the times Jesus used the word "repent" in the book of Revelation, which will be examined later when the ministry of John the Apostle is considered.

To Unbelievers

At the Beginning of His Ministry

According to Mathew and Mark, Jesus preached repentance from the very beginning of His ministry.

Same as John Matthew says that when Jesus began to preach, His message was, "Repent, for the kingdom of heaven is at hand" (Mt. 4:17). Since this statement is identical to the one concerning John the Baptist (Mt. 3:2), what Jesus meant by repent is the same thing John meant. What John meant by repentance was that people should change their thinking from trusting their merit before God to trusting the Messiah for the remission of sins (see the previous chapter). *No. Jesus offered the Kgdm*

To illustrate this method of interpretation, in the book of Acts, the first time Luke writes about tongues he describes tongues in detail (Acts 2:4-11). He clearly indicates that tongues are languages (Acts 2:6, 8, 9-11). On the other two occasions in the book of Acts when Luke refers to tongues (Acts 10:46; 19:6), he uses the same terminology. Therefore, it is reasonable to assume that in those passages, tongues means languages. The nature of communication is such that once authors define a term, they are obligated to use that term the same way, until they notify the readers otherwise. If that were not the case, communication would be meaningless. Thus, when Matthew first uses the word "repent," he includes clues as to what he means and it is safe to assume that is the way he is using the word the next time it appears.

Good News of Kgdm offer Mark says that when Jesus began to preach, His message was, "Repent and believe in the gospel" (Mk. 1:15). There are two issues here. First, what is the meaning of repentance? Mark does not record enough information *in this passage* to answer that question based on this context, but there is no reason to conclude that Mark meant something different concerning repentance than Matthew meant. Both are reporting the message of Jesus at the beginning of His ministry. Indeed, it would be highly unlikely, if not impossible, for Mark to have a different definition of repentance for John and Jesus than Matthew presented for them.

The other issue raised by Mark 1:15 is the relationship between "repent" and "believe." This is one of three places in the New Testament where repent and believe appear together (see Acts 20:21; Heb. 6:1). When repentance and faith are listed together, they are not exactly synonymous, but in that they sometimes stand alone as the requirement for salvation, they cannot be separated. When repentance occurs alone it includes faith and when faith occurs alone it implies repentance. So, when the forgiveness of sins is the subject, repentance and faith are inseparable. In Acts 20:21, repentance and faith are united by one article. Therefore, repentance and faith are not two steps to salvation; they are not temporally successive. They cannot be separated; but they ought to be distinguished (see the chapter on "The Meaning of Repentance").

Thus, John the Baptist proclaimed repent (Mt. 3:2) and believe (Acts 19:4) and so did Jesus (Mk. 1:15). John the Baptist meant change your thinking from trusting your merit to trusting the Messiah for the remission of sins. Jesus meant change your mind about trusting yourself (see below on Mt. 9:9-10) and believe the good news about Him (Mk. 1:15; the gospel is believing the good news about Jesus Christ; see Mk. 1:1). Again, they both proclaimed the same message.

At the Call of Matthew

Shortly after He called Matthew, a tax collector, Jesus ate with tax collectors and sinners (Mt. 9:9-10). The Pharisees complained to His disciples, "Why does your Teacher eat with tax collectors and sinners?" (Mt. 9:11). It is important to note that this criticism came from the Pharisees. In answer to the complaint of the Pharisees, Jesus said, "Those who are well have no need of a physician, but those who are sick" (Mt. 9:12). He went on to say, "For I did not come to call the righteous, but sinners, to repentance" (Mt. 9:13). This incident is repeated in Mark and Luke. Mark records that Jesus said, "Those who are well have no need of a physician, but those who are sick. I did not come to call *the* righteous, but sinners, to repentance" (Mk. 2:17) and Luke writes, Jesus said, "I have not come to call *the* righteous, but sinners, to repentance" (Lk. 5:32).

Since these remarks are in answer to the Pharisees, in order to understand what Jesus is saying here, it is imperative to understand what Jesus thought of them. On another occasion, He revealed what He thought: "Also He spoke this parable to some who trusted in themselves that they were righteous, and despised others. Two men went up to the temple to pray, one a Pharisee and the other a tax collector. The Pharisee stood and prayed thus with himself, 'God, I thank You that I am not like other men; extortioners, unjust, adulterers, or even as this tax collector. I fast twice a week; I give tithes of all that I possess.' And the tax collector, standing afar off, would not so much as raise his eyes to heaven, but beat his breast, saying, 'God, be merciful to me a sinner!' I tell you, this man went down to his house justified rather than the other; for everyone who exalts himself will be humbled, and he who humbles himself will be exalted" (Lk. 18:9-14).

In other words, Jesus thought that the Pharisees were trusting in themselves that they were righteous (Lk. 18:9) and that instead they needed to trust God's mercy (Lk. 18:13). That is what is going on in Matthew 9:9-10. Jesus is saying that the Pharisees felt that they were righteous (M'Neile). They did not feel that they needed a physician or a savior. They did not need God's mercy.

Jesus is also saying that He came to call sinners to repentance. He is calling them to change their minds about trusting themselves (as all sinners do) to recognizing that they need a savior. Being sick and needing a doctor is a good illustration of what the Lord means by repentance. As sick people need to recognize that they are sick, that they can not heal themselves, and that they need to trust a doctor to be healed, so, sinners need to recognize their spiritual sickness, sin, their inability to save themselves, and trust Him who heals spiritual disease.

To the Cities

A little later in Jesus' ministry, Matthew says, "Then He began to rebuke the cities in which most of His mighty works had been done, because they did not repent. 'Woe to you, Chorazin! Woe to you, Bethsaida! For if the mighty works which were done in you had been done in Tyre and Sidon, they would have repented long ago in sackcloth and ashes'" (Mt. 11:20-22).

Even though He did miracles in their midst, the Jews did not believe Jesus was the Messiah. Furthermore, they thought that they were righteous compared to the Gentiles. Jesus is saying that had Gentile cities seen the miracles that He had done in Jewish cities, they would have repented. In other words, the miracles that Jesus had done, had not changed the minds of the Jews about Jesus, but had the Gentiles seen these miracles they would have changed their mind about Him and they would have believed in Him.

Luke records that Jesus said, "Woe to you, Chorazin! Woe to you, Bethsaida! For if the mighty works which were done in you had been done in Tyre and Sidon, they would have repented long ago, sitting in sackcloth and ashes" (Lk. 10:13). As in Matthew's account, the Jews thought that they were better than the Gentiles, but Jesus is saying that if He had done mighty miracles in Tyre and Sidon, Gentile cities, the people in those cities (Gentiles) would have changed their minds about Him and they would have sat around in sackcloth and ashes. Sitting in sackcloth and ashes is "an attendant emotional response, which would have occurred subsequent to (their) change of attitude" (Wilkin, dissertation, p. 47). It was the fruit of repentance, like the Ninevites who changed their minds (Jonah 3:5a) and as a result put on sackcloth and ashes and turned from their wicked ways (Jonah 3:5b-9).

To those Seeking a Sign

Some of the scribes and Pharisees said to Jesus, "Teacher, we want to see a sign from You" (Mt. 12:38). Jesus said that "the men of Nineveh will rise up in the judgment with this generation and condemn it, because they repented at the preaching of Jonah; and indeed a greater than Jonah *is* here" (Mt. 12:41).

In Matthew 11:21-22, Jesus gave a hypothetical comparison. Now He gives an actual case, the case of the Ninevites, who repented at the preaching of Jonah. The way the word "repent" has been used in Matthew so far and especially the way it is used of a similar situation in Matthew 11:21-22 suggests that "repent" here is a change of mind. Moreover, what the book of Jonah says is that "the people of Nineveh believed God" (Jonah 3:5). "Their repentance consisted in believing in God" and "their subsequent turning from their wicked way (Jonah 3:6-10) was the fruit of their repentance and not the repentance itself" (Wilkin, dissertation, p. 110-111).

Luke records, "And while the crowds were thickly gathered together, He began to say, 'This is an evil generation. It seeks a sign, and no sign will be given to it except the sign of Jonah the prophet. For as Jonah became a sign to the Ninevites, so also the Son of Man will be to this generation. The queen of the South will rise up in the judgment with the men of this generation and condemn them, for she came from the ends of the earth to hear the wisdom of Solomon; and indeed a greater than Solomon is here. The men of Nineveh will rise up in the judgment with this generation and condemn it, for they repented at the preaching of Jonah; and indeed a greater than Jonah is here'" (Lk. 11:29-32).

Jesus had done miracles in their midst, but they attributed His miracles to the work of Satan (Lk. 11:14-15). They "sought from Him a sign from heaven" (Lk. 11:16). Jesus declares that they were "spiritually corrupt" and, therefore, they demanded "an extraordinary" sign "to prove conclusively that He was indeed the Messiah" (Geldenhuys). They wanted "direct testimony from God Himself. . . . such as a voice from heaven or a pillar of fire." They wanted to be "miraculously convinced" (Plummer).

Jesus says that they would not be given any other signs, except the sign of Jonah. Luke omits the explanation that Jonah was a type of the death and resurrection of Christ (Mt. 12:40), but that explanation is implied (Plummer).

He then adds that the Queen of the South, a Gentile, came from the ends of the earth to hear Solomon. There are a number of contrasts here: 1) between a Gentile Queen and the Jews, 2) between the ends of the earth and here, 3) between Solomon and the Son of Man, and perhaps, 4) between a woman and men (Plummer), but the point is that "she believed the report she heard" while the Jews "rejected Him in their unbelief" (Geldenhuys). Her response is a condemnation of the response of the Jews. To make matters worse, One greater than Solomon was present.

Jesus goes on to say that the people of Nineveh repented at the preaching of Jonah. Again, Gentiles readily responded, whereas the Jewish generation did not. They "hardened themselves in unbelief" (Geldenhuys). So, the response of the people of Nineveh is a condemnation of the response of the Jewish generation of Jesus' day. Again, to make matters worse One greater than Jonah was in their midst.

The repentance in Luke 11:32 is changing one's mind about Christ. The Jews did not believe He was the Messiah. In contrast, the Queen of the South came "to hear the wisdom of Solomon"

(Lk. 11:31) and she accepted what he said. The people of Nineveh repented. That is, they accepted Jonah as a messenger from God and "believed God" (Jonah 3:5). Jesus was calling His audience "to accept Him and His message before it was too late" (Wilkin, dissertation, p. 48).

At the Falling of the Tower

The Galileans thought that people who experienced a calamity must be extremely sinful (Lk. 13:1-2, 4), implying that they were not sinful, or at least, as sinful as they were. During Jesus' day, people believed that disaster was a punishment for sin (Jn. 9:2; see Morris). According to these Galileans, a "calamity was the judgment upon the sufferers for exceptional wickedness" (Plummer). God allowed people to be overtaken by such disasters because they were "exceptionally sinful" (Geldenhuys). Extraordinary calamity was an indication of exceptional sin.

Jesus told them, "I tell you, no; but unless you repent you will all likewise perish" (Lk. 13:3; He says the same thing again in verse 5). He insists that these people had not been "singled out for a horrible death because they were worse sinners than others" (Morris). He reminds them that they are all sinners (Plummer) seizing the opportunity to tell them that they need to "repent." In this context, "repent" obviously means to change your mind about who you are. You are a sinner who needs a savior. *? or chg of mind about Xp*

At the Complaint of the Pharisees

Later in Christ's ministry, the Pharisees again complained when Jesus ate with sinners (Lk. 15:1-2; see 5:30). In reply, Jesus told three stories, apparently considered one parable (Lk. 15:3). He said, "I say to you that likewise there will be more joy in heaven over one sinner who repents than over ninety-nine just persons who need no repentance" (Lk. 15:7-twice). "Likewise, I say to you, there is joy in the presence of the angels of God over one sinner who repents" (Lk. 15:10).

The first story is about a lost sheep (Lk. 15:4-7). The Pharisees had a saying, "There is joy before God when those who provoke Him perish from the world" (Plummer). Jesus says, on the contrary, there is more joy in heaven over one sinner who repents than over ninety-nine people who need no repentance (Lk. 15:7).

The second story is about a lost coin. This time instead of saying there is joy in heaven, Jesus speaks of "joy in the presence of the angels of God" (Lk. 15:10). In contrast to the Pharisees who complained (Lk. 15:2), the "angelic estimate" is very different (Plummer). In the presence of angels, there is joy. The point is the same as the one made in verse 7, namely, in contrast to the Pharisees who saw no need for God's mercy, sinners, those who recognize their sinfulness and need for God's mercy, cause rejoicing in heaven.

The third story is about a lost son. The fact that the story is about a prodigal *son* has prompted some to conclude that this is about a believer coming back to the Lord (Chafer, vol. I, p. 244). This is a parable, a form of literature designed to teach one basic truth. While some of the details in parables may have significance, not all details necessarily do. In this case, the context and content of the passage indicate that Jesus is using a father–son relationship as an illustration of sinners being saved. Jesus is answering the complaint that He was eating with *sinners* (Lk. 15:1). The son was said to be *dead* and *lost* (Lk. 15:32). The word repent is not used in this story, but obviously, the prodigal changed his mind. The real point of this story is that the older brother was out of sympathy with the father, a picture of the self-righteous attitude of the Pharisees.

With a self-righteous attitude, the Pharisees were thinking they were better than others and able to enter the kingdom on the basis of their own law-keeping righteousness (Lk. 18:9). The contrast in this passage is not between righteous people and people living in sin. It is between self-righteous people, who feel no need for repentance, and sinners who are much more likely to change their minds about themselves and realize their need for God's forgiveness. Repentance in this passage is a change of mind from a self-righteous attitude that does not see a need for God's mercy to an attitude of realizing one's sinfulness and therefore a need for God's forgiveness.

Commenting on this passage, Geldenhuys says, "In no other religion in the whole world does one come to know God as the One who in His love seeks the lost person to save him through His grace. In the writings of other religions we see how man seeks and yearns for God, but in the Bible we see how God in Christ seeks man to save him for time and eternity. Because the Savior has paid with His precious blood for the redemption of man, every soul has an infinite value in God's sight and the way to the throne of grace lies open to everyone who desires to enter."

In the Story about Lazarus

In the story Jesus told about a rich man and a beggar named Lazarus, the rich man in hades said to Abraham, "I beg you therefore, father, that you would send him (Lazarus) to my father's house, for I have five brothers, that he may testify to them, lest they also come to this place of torment" (Lk. 16:27-28). When "Abraham said to him, 'They have Moses and the prophets; let them hear them'" (Lk. 16:29), the rich man said, "No, father Abraham; but if one goes to them from the dead, they will repent" (Lk. 16:30). "But he (Abraham) said to him (the rich man), 'If they do not hear Moses and the prophets, neither will they be persuaded though one rise from the dead'" (Lk. 16:31). Abraham said they had the Scripture, which they should "hear" (Lk. 16:29), meaning they had the Scripture that speaks about Christ and they should believe in Him. Moses (cf. Deut. 18:15) and the prophets (cf. Isa. 52:13-53:12; Dan. 7:13-14, 27) predicted the coming of the Messiah, yet when He came, the nation refused to believe in Him.

In his reply to Abraham, the rich man used "repent" in place of "hear" (Lk. 16:30) and, when Abraham responds, he says that if they will not "hear" the Scripture, they will not be "persuaded though one rise from the dead" (Lk. 16:31). That was prophetic, because even after Jesus was raised from the dead people did not believe, but the point here is that Abraham linked "hear" with "repent" and added "persuaded" as well. Thus, "repent" in this passage is listening to the Scripture and believing in Jesus.

At the End of His Ministry

After His resurrection, Jesus said, "Thus it is written, and thus it was necessary for the Christ to suffer and to rise from the dead the third day, and that repentance and remission of sins should be preached in His name to all nations, beginning at Jerusalem" (Lk. 24:46-47). The phrase "in His name" connects the preaching of repentance and remission with His death and resurrection (Morris).

Based on Christ's fulfillment of the Old Testament prophecies concerning His death and resurrection, the disciples were to preach repentance and remission of sins to all nations. Israel had been instrumental in having Jesus killed. Now it was to be preached that their Scriptures were fulfilled in Him and they were to change their minds about Him in order to be forgiven. It is clear that is what Jesus meant and that is what the disciples understood from Peter's sermons in Acts.

Concerning Believers

On one occasion Jesus used the word "repent" of a believer, instead of an unbeliever. He said, "Take heed to yourselves. If your brother sins against you, rebuke him; and if he repents, forgive him. And if he sins against you seven times in a day, and seven times in a day returns to you, saying, 'I repent,' you shall forgive him" (Lk. 17:3-4). Jesus says that if a brother (fellow believer) sins against you, you should *rebuke* him, which obviously means talk to him. You are to "call his attention to his wrong behavior (and not slander him behind his back!)" (Geldenhuys).

If the brother who has sinned against you repents, you are to forgive him, even if he sins seven times in one day and seven times says, "I repent." The seven times is not to be taken literally (Plummer), as if to say on the eight time you are not forgiven (Morris). Elsewhere Jesus made that clear (Mt. 18:21-22). The point is unlimited forgiveness (Plummer).

What is the nature of repentance in this passage? The repentance is apparently not a change in behavior, because the brother sins seven times in one day. It is in something he says (cf. "saying"). Based on the Lord's use of "repent" in the book of Luke prior to this verse, it is reasonable to assume that the repentance here is like the one who sinned saying, "by what you said (cf. 'rebuke'), I see your point and you are right; I change my mind about what I have done." As one commentator put it, "The pardon to be granted to our brethren has no other limit than their repenting, and the confession by which it is expressed" (Godet).

Summary: When Jesus used the word "repent," He meant change your mind from trusting your righteousness to trusting God's mercy or change your mind about who He is.

Imbedded in the message to change your mind about trusting your righteousness before God is the idea that you must trust someone (or something) else. So, to people who trusted their righteousness before God (Lk. 18:9), Jesus preached repentance, that is, a change of mind *from* trusting their righteousness *to* trusting God's mercy (Lk. 18:13). He also used the word "repent" to mean "change your mind" concerning who He is.

Would it be possible for people to realize that they should not trust their own righteousness and still not trust the righteousness of Christ? When people are trusting their own efforts to obtain salvation and repent (change their minds about that), they of necessity have to place their faith somewhere else. The gospel is the message that faith for salvation is to be placed in Jesus Christ. Wilkin concludes that, while that may be logically possible, Luke does not seem to conceive of "someone recognizing his sinfulness and need of grace and forgiveness and then refusing to believe in Jesus Christ." Wilkin adds that as far as Luke is concerned "true repentance" leads to faith in Christ" (Wilkin, dissertation, p. 62).

"Repentance is not opposed to grace; it is the recognition of the need of grace" (Ironside, p. 10). "Repentance is the sinner's recognition of and acknowledgment of his lost state and, thus, of his need of grace" (Ironside, p. 11).

When Dave Drummond, a fellow pastor and a dear friend, read this manuscript and got to this point, he suggested that I should say that repentance is a transfer of trust from self-righteousness to the Savior. That says it well, very well.

Chapter 5

THE MESSAGE OF PETER

John the Baptist and Jesus the Christ preached repentance. When John used the word, he meant change your mind from trusting your merit to trusting the Messiah. When Jesus used the word, He meant change your mind from trusting your own righteousness to trusting God's mercy or change your mind about who He is. John and Jesus are not the only ones to preach repentance. Jesus commissioned His disciples to preach repentance. Actually, He did that twice.

Mark 6:12

During His ministry, His disciples preached repentance. Mark says that the disciples "went out and preached that people should repent" (Mk. 6:12). This is the only reference in the synoptic gospels to the disciples preaching repentance. There is not sufficient information in the immediate context to determine what the disciples meant by "repent." No details are given. Since Mark did not explain what the disciples said about "repent," it is safe to assume that they meant by it what Jesus meant by it. After all, they were His disciples! Lane (and others) reached the same conclusion. He says the disciples preached "the message of repentance which Jesus preached."

Luke 24:47

After His resurrection, Jesus said, "Thus it is written, and thus it was necessary for the Christ to suffer and to rise from the dead the third day, and that repentance and remission of sins should be preached in His name to all nations, beginning at Jerusalem" (Lk. 24:46-47). The disciples were to preach the death and resurrection of Christ and the remission of sins. In other words, they were to tell people that in order to receive the remission of sins, they had to repent; that is, change their minds about Jesus Christ who died for sin.

The book of Acts records what the disciples did as a result of that commission. How did these disciples use the word repentance? Actually, Acts is about the acts of Peter and Paul. How did they preach repentance?

Of the fifty-eight appearances of the terms "repent" and "repentance" in the New Testament, six are related to Peter. He told people to repent (Acts 2:38; 3:19; 5:31; 8:22); others said that is what happened when he preached on one occasion (Acts 11:18) and he said God wanted all to repent (2 Pet. 3:9).

To Unbelievers

Acts 2:38

On the day of Pentecost, Peter preached the death and resurrection of Christ to the Jews at Jerusalem (Acts 2:22-35). In the process, he said, "You have taken by lawless hands, have crucified, and put to death" (Acts 2:23) the Messiah and "this Jesus, whom you crucified, (is) both Lord and Christ" (Acts 2:36). Notice, Peter said, "You crucified" (Acts 2:23, 36). He made them personally responsible.

Luke records, "Now when they heard *this*, they were cut to the heart, and said to Peter and the rest of the apostles, 'Men *and* brethren, what shall we do?'" (Acts 2:37). In response, "Peter said to them, 'Repent, and let every one of you be baptized in the name of Jesus Christ for the remission of sins; and you shall receive the gift of the Holy Spirit'" (Acts 2:38).

In the context of this sermon, the issue is not their personal sins of sexual immorality or stealing. It is their attitude about Christ. Peter charged his listeners with thinking that Christ was a common criminal. He tells them to "repent," that is, change their minds concerning Christ. "From regarding Him as an impostor, a false Christ, they were now to believe on Him as the true Messiah" (Gloag, who pours more into the word "repent" than the text warrants, at least understands that the word "repent" in this context is a change of mind about Christ).

Notice carefully what is going on in this passage. The people in Jerusalem thought of Jesus as a mere man worthy of death. Peter proclaims Him to be the Messiah, who died and arose, and tells them to "repent," that is, change their minds about Him, so that they could receive the remission of sins. Therefore, by "repent," Peter is saying that they must change their opinion concerning Christ and trust Him for forgiveness.

Peter also says, "Let every one of you be baptized in the name of Jesus Christ for the remission of sins." It sounds like Peter is saying that baptism is necessary for the remission of sins, but elsewhere baptism is never said to be the condition of the remission of sins. So, what does the expression "be baptized in the name of Jesus Christ for the remission of sins" mean? Two explanations are possible.

In the Greek text "repent" is in the plural, "baptize" is in the singular and "receive" is in the plural. The change from the plural to the singular and back to plural again suggests that the baptism clause may be parenthetical. If so, Peter is saying that the condition of the remission of sins is repentance. Baptism follows forgiveness.

On the other hand, the distance of the forgiveness phrase from the word "repent" and its closeness to baptism seems to suggest that the remission of sin is connected to baptism. That does not mean Peter is saying, "Be baptized *in order to* get remission." It could mean he is telling them, "Be baptized *because* your sins have been remitted."

In support of this view is that fact that throughout Luke's writings in both his gospel and the book of Acts repentance, not baptism, is the condition of remission (Lk. 3:3; 13:3, 5; 24:47; Acts 3:19; 5:31; 11:18; 17:30-31; 20:18, 20). Furthermore, the Greek word translated "for" (*eis*) in the expression "for the remission of sins" can mean "because." The people of Nineveh repented "at" (*eis*) the preaching of Jonah" (Mt. 12:41). They did not repent in order to get the preaching of Jonah, but because of his preaching (see comments on Mt. 3:11, esp. Dana and Mantey, p. 104).

John the Baptist preached repentance as the condition of forgiveness and baptism as a sign that one had repented (see comments on Mt. 3:11). After Pentecost, Peter told people to "repent" so that their sins might be blotted out (Acts 3:19); but he made no mention of baptism. In Acts 10:34-43, Peter preached that the condition of forgiveness is faith. The people who heard him were forgiven before baptism was even mentioned (Acts 10:44-48).

To sum up, Peter told the people in Jerusalem on the day of Pentecost that they needed to repent for the remission of sins and be baptized because their sins had been forgiven. In other words, "repent" in this passage means to change your mind about Christ and trust Him for forgiveness. So, baptism here is an "expression of repentance" (F. F. Bruce; see also Marshall).

In his book, *The Great Doctrines of the Bible*, Williams Evans says, "Thus, when Peter, on the day of Pentecost, called upon the Jews to repent (Acts 2:14-40), he virtually called upon them to change their minds and their views regarding Christ. They had considered Christ to be a mere man, a blasphemer, an impostor. The events of the few preceding days had proven to them that He was none other than the righteous Son of God, their Savior and the Savior of the world. The result of their repentance or change of mind would be that they would receive Jesus Christ as their long promised Messiah" (Evans, p. 140).

Ryrie concurs. He writes, "But if repentance means changing your mind about the particular sin of rejecting Christ, then that kind of repentance saves, and of course it is the same as faith in Christ. This is what Peter asked the crowd to do on the day of Pentecost. They were to change their minds about Jesus of Nazareth. Formerly they had considered Him to be only a blasphemous human being claiming to be God; now they changed their minds and saw Him as the God-man Savior whom they would trust for salvation. That kind of repentance saves, and everyone who is saved has repented in that sense" (Ryrie, *A Survey of Bible Doctrine*, p. 139). *This is wrong repent can no way saves - ever.*

No → it is to belief in Xp

Acts 3:19

At the Temple in Jerusalem, Peter preached the death and resurrection of Christ to the Jews (Acts 3:13-15, 18, 26). As in the sermon in Acts 2, Peter again not only preached the death and resurrection of Christ, he also charged the Jews at Jerusalem with the personal responsibility in the death of Christ (cf.

"you" in 3:13 and 14). Again, he concluded, "Repent therefore and be converted, that your sins may be blotted out, so that times of refreshing may come from the presence of the Lord" (Acts 3:19). In the context of Peter's sermon in Acts 3, "repent" in Acts 3 is the same as in Acts 2, namely, that they change their minds about Christ. "All they had to do to avail themselves of this salvation was to change their former attitude to Jesus and bring it into line with God's attitude. God had clearly declared his verdict by raising him from the dead" (F. F. Bruce).

This time Peter adds "and be converted," a Greek word which means, "turn." They were to change their minds about Christ and turn to the Lord (see Acts 26:20, where this same Greek for turn is used and "to God" is added, indicating that the turning is to God).

In the book of Acts (and elsewhere), when "turning" is used of salvation, it means turning to the Lord, which is the same as trusting Christ. In Acts 9, Peter healed a man and all who saw it "turned to the Lord" (Acts 9:35), but a little later in the passage, Luke's comments on that event is that "many believed in the Lord" (Acts 9:42).

Acts 11:21 says that "a great number believed and turned to the Lord." The word "and" is not in the Greek text. The word "turn" is a command and the word "believed" is a participle. Wilkin calls the participle a circumstantial participle of manner, meaning the manner in which they turned to the Lord was by believing (Wilkin, dissertation, p. 220).

In Acts 14:15, Paul said that he preached "that you should turn from these useless things (idols) to the living God, who made the heaven, the earth, the sea, and all things that are in them." Luke's comment was that the people who turned from idols to the living God, "believed" (Acts 14:23). Therefore, turning from idols to the living God is believing in Jesus Christ.

At the Jerusalem Council, James spoke of the Gentiles "turning to God" (Acts 15:19). In the context of the discussion at that council, there can be no doubt that "turning to God" is another expression of trusting in Christ. Peter says the Gentiles were to "hear the word of the gospel and believe" (Acts 15:7) and God purified "their hearts by faith" (Acts 15:9). He added that "we believe that through the grace of the Lord Jesus Christ we shall be saved in the same manner as they" (Acts 15:11). James is agreeing with what Peter said (Acts 15:14-15) and therefore his expression "turning to God" is another way of speaking about believing the gospel.

In Acts 26, Paul explains to Agrippa that Christ told him "to open their eyes, *in order* to turn *them* from darkness to light, and *from* the power of Satan to God, that they may receive forgiveness of sins and an inheritance among those who are sanctified by faith in Me" (Acts 26:18). Then he tells Agrippa that he preached "they should repent, turn to God, and do works befitting repentance" (Acts 26:20). To turn from darkness to light, and from the power of Satan to God (Acts 26:18) and to turn to God (Acts 26:20) is to trust Christ, which is clear from the expression "by faith in Me" at the end of verse 18.

No — Turning is synonymous with believing in John 12:40 (and therefore, in Mt. 13:15; Mk. 4:12; and Acts 28:27), where John says that people "could not believe, because Isaiah said" (Jn. 12:39) "He has blinded their eyes and hardened their hearts, lest they should see with their eyes, lest they should understand with their hearts and turn, so that I should heal them" (Jn. 12:40). What Isaiah calls turning, John calls believing. When some did not believe what Paul was preaching concerning Christ (Acts 28:23-24), like John, Luke quotes Isaiah 6, indicating that turning in Isaiah is believing in Christ. *in order to bel in Xp*

People turn (or turn to the Lord or turn to God) by believing in Jesus Christ.

To sum up, Peter told the people at the Temple in Jerusalem that they need to repent; that is, change their minds about Christ, and trust Jesus Christ so that their sins would be blotted out. In other words, "repent and turn" in this passage means to change your mind about Christ and trust Him for forgiveness.

Yes ! In *Basic Theology*, Ryrie says, "This saving repentance has to involve a change of mind about Jesus Christ so that whatever a *Context?* person thought of Him before, he changes his mind ⟨and⟩ trusts Him to be his Savior" (Ryrie, *Basic Theology*, p. 337).

Acts 5:31

Before the Jewish Sanhedrin in Jerusalem, Peter preached the death and resurrection of Christ (Acts 5:30). As in his two previous sermons recorded in Acts (Acts 2 and 3), Peter charged the Jewish leaders with being guilty of murdering Christ (Acts

5:28, 30). Even though they were guilty of murdering Christ, Peter tells them, "Him God has exalted to His right hand to be Prince and Savior, to give repentance to Israel and forgiveness of sins" (Acts 5:31). The situation (you killed Christ) and the solution (repentance) is the same as in Acts 2 and Acts 3. Therefore, the meaning of repentance in Acts 5:31 is the same as in Acts 2 and 3, namely, change your opinion concerning Christ and trust Him for forgiveness (Wilkin, dissertation, p. 75).

God giving Israel repentance (Acts 5:31) cannot mean that He gave the nation the gift of repentance. Only a few repented. Rather the expression "to give repentance to Israel" (Acts 5:31) means that God gave the people of Israel "the opportunity of repentance" (Marshall).

To sum up, Peter told the Sanhedrin that they need to repent, that is, change their minds about Jesus. Of course, if they changed their minds about Jesus, understanding that He died for sin and arose from the dead, they would trust Him for forgiveness. In other words, "repent" in this passage means to change your mind about Jesus and trust Him for forgiveness.

Acts 11:18

Peter preached the death and resurrection of Jesus to Gentiles at Cornelius' house (Acts 10:39-40). He told them, "Whoever believes in Him will receive remission of sins" (Acts 10:43). Then, "While Peter was still speaking these words, the Holy Spirit fell upon all those who heard the word" (Acts 10:44). In other words, in the middle of the sermon, the moment that they heard the message of forgiveness by faith in Jesus, they trusted Jesus, which is proven by the fact that the Holy Spirit fell on them.

This is the first time that Gentiles had trusted Jesus. When Peter got back to Jerusalem, Jewish believers "contended with him, saying, 'You went in to uncircumcised men and ate with them!'" (Acts 11:2-3). Peter had to explain his part in Gentiles coming to Christ, which he did (Acts 11:4-17). Peter concluded by saying, "If therefore God gave them the same gift as He gave us when we believed on the Lord Jesus Christ, who was I that I could withstand God?" (Acts 11:17). Notice, what the Gentiles did was believe in Jesus (Acts 10:43-44) and in reporting this to the believers at Jerusalem, Peter spoke of "when we believed on the Lord Jesus Christ" (Acts 11:17). Thus far in this story, nothing has been said about repentance.

Here is the response of the believers in Jerusalem: "When they heard these things they became silent; and they glorified God saying, 'Then God has also granted to the Gentiles repentance to life'" (Acts 11:18). God granting them repentance, means that He gave them an *opportunity* to repent (see comments on Acts 5:31 and also Marshall). One commentator remarks that they had "a change of mind and heart and assurance of eternal life" (F. F. Bruce).

Peter told the people assembled in Cornelius' house that whoever believes in Jesus receives the remission of sins (Acts 10:43). In reporting the incident to the Jews in Jerusalem, Peter said that the people in Cornelius' house received the same gift we did "when we believed on the Lord Jesus Christ" (Acts 11:17). Yet, the Jews in Jerusalem call what happened in Cornelius' house "repentance" (Acts 11:18). Therefore, what has been described as faith (Acts 10:43; 11:17) is now called repentance (Acts 11:18). *Not so. 2 diff things.*

In light of the fact that in his previous evangelistic sermons, Peter conditioned salvation for Jews solely on repentance, which in context is clearly changing one's attitude about Jesus Christ (cf. Acts 2:38, 3:19; 5:31), it can only be concluded that "Peter considered calling Jews to change their attitudes about Jesus Christ to be identical with calling Gentiles to faith in Him" (Wilkin, dissertation, p. 80). Moreover, since Luke does not cite Peter as mentioning repentance anywhere in this account (cf. Acts 10:34-11:17), the response of the Jewish believers at Jerusalem means that they considered "repentance unto life" (Acts 11:18) to be "conceptually parallel" with faith in Jesus Christ (Wilkin, dissertation, p. 81). Commenting on this passage, Chafer says "Repentance, which is included in believing, serves as a synonym for the word *belief*" (Chafer, vol. 3, p. 377).

Synecdoche of part for the whole.

2 Peter 3:9

In his second epistle Peter writes, "The Lord is not slack concerning His promise, as some count slackness, but is longsuffering toward us, not willing that any should perish but that all should come to repentance" (2 Pet. 3:9). There is no object for repentance expressed in this verse or implied in the context. Furthermore, this is the only occurrence of either the word "repent" or the word "repentance" in Peter's epistles.

Therefore, the only available evidence for determining the meaning of the word "repentance" by Peter is Peter's use of the word in the book of Acts. In the book of Acts the meaning of Peter's use of repentance is a change of mind about Jesus Christ (see comments on Acts 2:38; 3:19; 5:31; see also Wilkin, dissertation, p. 187).

To Believers

Acts 8:22

Philip went down to Samaria and preached Jesus (Acts 8:5). Simon, who had practiced sorcery, believed and was baptized (Acts 8:13). Then Peter and John arrived, laid hands on them, and they received the Holy Spirit (Acts 8:17). "When Simon saw that through the laying on of the apostles' hands the Holy Spirit was given, he offered them money saying, 'Give me this power also, that anyone on whom I lay hands may receive the Holy Spirit'" (Acts 8:19). "Peter said to him, 'Your money perish with you, because you thought that the gift of God could be purchased with money! You have neither part nor portion in this matter, for your heart is not right in the sight of God. Repent therefore of this your wickedness, and pray God if perhaps the thought of your heart may be forgiven you. For I see that you are poisoned by bitterness and bound by iniquity" (Acts 8:20-23).

Commentators differ over whether or not Simon was genuinely converted. The text says he believed and was baptized, which certainly indicates that he was genuinely regenerate. The problem is that the text also says that when he wanted to buy the power to lay hands on people and give them the Holy Spirit, Peter told him, "Your money perish with you" and "your heart is not right in the sight of God."

There is nothing in the text to suggest that Simon's faith and baptism were any different than the other Samaritans who were converted. The fact that he was told that he might "perish" does not necessarily mean that he was going to go to hell, because the Greek word translated "perish" is sometimes used of temporal destruction, ruin, or loss. It is used of "wasted" perfume (Mt. 26:8; Mk. 14:4), of capital punishment (Acts 25:16) and of believers who fall into the snare of the love of money (1 Tim. 6:9, cf. 6:10). The destruction to which Peter refers could be premature physical death (Acts 5:1-11; 1 Cor. 11:30; Jas. 5:19-20; 1 Jn. 5:16-17; see Wilkin, dissertation, pp. 77-78).

Be all that as it may, it is evident from the text that what Peter meant by "repent" was a change of mind. Simon had not *done* anything in terms of behavior; he *thought* he could buy the power to lay hands on people so that they could receive the Holy Spirit (Acts 8:20). Peter plainly says, "*Your heart* is not right in the sight of God" (Acts 8:21) and that his problem was the *thought* of his heart (Acts 8:22). In this case, however, the change of mind is not an unbeliever changing his mind about Jesus. It is a believer changing his mind about buying the power to lay hands on people so that they could receive the Holy Spirit.

Summary: Peter's message of repentance was that people should change their minds about Jesus (Acts 2:38; 3:19; 5:31); and implied in that message is that they should also trust Him. He also told a believer to change his mind about what he was thinking concerning buying the ministry of the Holy Spirit.

Peter charged the Jews at Jerusalem with the murder of Jesus Christ. In telling them to repent, he was telling them to reverse their attitude about Jesus Christ from viewing Jesus as a common criminal to acknowledging Him as the Messiah. Like Jesus and John the Baptist, Peter promised the forgiveness of sins for those who repented (cf. Lk. 3:3; 5:32; 16:30; 24:47; Acts 2:38; 3:19; 5:31).

In his only sermon to Gentiles, Peter called his listeners to believe in Jesus and made no mention of repentance. Apparently, Peter considered calling Jews to change their minds about Jesus to be "conceptually parallel" with calling Gentiles to faith in Him (cf. Acts 10:34 with 11:18; see, Wilkin, dissertation, p. 81-82). It is "reasonable" to conclude that Peter equated repentance, that is, changing one's mind about Christ, with believing in Christ (Wilkin, *JOTGES*, Spring 1990, p. 17).

Chapter 6

THE MESSAGE OF PAUL

L ike John the Baptist, Jesus, and Peter, Paul preached repentance. In the book of Acts he mentions it six times (twice in Acts 26:20). Two of the six are references to the ministry of John the Baptist (Acts 13:24; 19:4; see the chapter on the Ministry of John the Baptist). Paul speaks of repentance five times in his epistles.

In the Book of Acts

Acts 17:30

At Athens, Paul spoke to a gathering of idol worshippers. He told them, "Therefore, since we are the offspring of God, we ought not to think that the Divine Nature is like gold or silver or stone, something shaped by art and man's devising. Truly, these times of ignorance God overlooked, but now commands all men everywhere to repent" (Acts 17:29-30). Notice, Paul said, they ought not to "think" God is like an idol (Acts 17:29). He also said that their problem was "ignorance" (Acts 17:30). Paul then moved quickly to talking about Jesus Christ and His resurrection (Acts 17:31) at which point he was interrupted (Acts 17:32). The episode ends with Luke saying that some "believed" (Acts 17:34).

From what is said in this passage, it is evident that when Paul uses the word "repent" (Acts 17:30), he means "change your mind" about the nature of God; idols are not actually gods and implied in it (as a result) is "trust Jesus Christ." One commentator says Paul told them to "repent: to change their mind and their views, to renounce their idolatries" (Gloag). Another says that Paul is saying they are to repent "of their false concept of God (and consequent flouting of his will) and embrace the true knowledge of his being made available in the Gospel" (F. F. Bruce). In other words, Paul called idolaters to change their minds from faith in idols to faith in Jesus Christ. The call to change one's attitude concerning idols and God is essentially equivalent to a call to faith in Christ (see Wilkin, dissertation, p. 121).

Acts 20:21

In his farewell address to the elders at Ephesus, Paul described his ministry as "testifying to Jews, and also to Greeks, repentance toward God and faith toward our Lord Jesus Christ" (Acts 20:21). The object of repentance here is God. Paul preached that people had to change their minds about God (cf. Acts 17:30). Toussaint says, "In the Greek the words repent and faith are joined together by one article. This may imply that these two words stress two aspects of trust in Christ (cf. 2:38). When a person places his faith in Christ, he is then turning from (repenting of) his former unbelief" (Toussaint).

This is one of only three places in the New Testament where repentance and faith appear together. The other two are Mark 1:15 and Hebrews 6:1. In the Greek text of Acts 20:21, one article unites both repentance and faith. The meaning is that Paul called both Jews and Gentiles to change their thinking about and have faith in God and the Lord Jesus Christ (Wilkin, who points out that in the Majority text there is a second article, but it functions as a pronoun, dissertation, pp. 90-91). Hence, repentance and faith cannot be separated; they are inseparable, but they can be distinguished (see comments on Mk. 1:15).

Acts 26:20 (twice)

Paul told Agrippa that Christ sent him to the Gentiles (Acts 26:15-17) "to open their eyes and to turn them from darkness to light, and from the power of Satan to God, that they may receive forgiveness of sins, and an inheritance among those, who are sanctified by faith that is in Me" (Acts 26:18). In short, Paul was sent to preach forgiveness of sins through faith in Jesus Christ.

Addressing Agrippa by name, Paul then says that he was obedient. He says that he "declared first to those in Damascus and in Jerusalem, and throughout all the region of Judea, and then to the Gentiles, that they should repent, turn to God, and do works befitting repentance" (Acts 26:20). In the context of Paul's speech, "repent, turn to God" in verse 20 is the same as faith in Christ in verse 18, because verse 19 and 20 are an explanation of verse 18 (Wilkin, dissertation, p. 90). Ironside says that Paul is simply insisting that sick people must recognize and acknowledge the incurableness of their terrible disease, so far as human help is concerned, in order that they may cast themselves in faith upon the Great Physician (Ironside, pp. 62-63).

It is obvious that repentance and turning to God are internal attitudes, because they are followed by *works* befitting the repentance, which are clearly external acts of behavior. As in Luke 3:8, there is no doubt that here there is a difference between repentance, an internal change of mind, and works, an external change of conduct. The "subsequent way of life" shows the "genuineness" of repentance (F. F. Bruce). It is the "practical evidence" of repentance (Marshall).

Paul's message of repentance was consistent with, not contradictory to, the preaching of repentance by John the Baptist, Jesus, and Peter. Granted, Paul's message was distinctive, in that he told people to change their minds about idols (the nature of God), but his message was not different in substance. All used repentance as a change of attitude in order to be forgiven.

In His Epistles

Romans 2:4

Paul begins the body of the book of Romans with the declaration that "the wrath of God is revealed from heaven against all ungodliness and unrighteousness" (Rom. 1:18). He proceeds to demonstrate that people have rejected the knowledge of God and consequently, God in His wrath has given them over to sin (Rom. 1:19-32). After that Paul introduces a self-righteous man who thinks that he is so righteous that he judges others (Rom. 2:1). When I taught Romans, I entitled this section "But I'm Righteous."

(handwritten margin note: this is not prophecy that they will do the same sin, but tells us that if they judge for a sin they will suffer the discipline for that sin.)

Paul responded to this self-righteous individual by saying that people who judge others condemn themselves, because they commit what they condemn (Rom. 2:1). If the sin people criticize is worthy of judgment, and they who condemn it in others, do it, they condemn themselves and are inexcusable.

Paul goes on to explain that judgment is according to truth (Rom. 2:2). Nevertheless, the self-righteous think they will escape the judgment of God (Rom. 2:3). Self-righteous people who judge others think that they are righteous and will somehow escape the judgment of God.

In the process of condemning others, the self-righteous not only do not see the same fault in themselves or think that they will be judged, but they spurn the opportunity they have to repent themselves. So Paul asks, "Or do you despise the riches of His goodness, forbearance, and longsuffering, not knowing that the goodness of God leads you to repentance?" (Rom. 2:4). In his commentary on Romans, William R. Newell writes, "Furthermore, such a 'judge' of others becomes, in his self-confident importance, blind to God's constant mercy toward himself—not feeling the need of it; and in his self-righteous blindness knows not that the 'goodness' of God is meant to lead him to personal repentance instead of the judgment of his fellows."

God's goodness should lead self-righteous people to repent, that is, change their mind about their self-righteousness and see their need for forgiveness (see Wilkin, dissertation, p. 124-126). To suggest that repentance here is "forsaking of sin, and turning from it" (Barnes) would be to repudiate everything Paul teaches in Romans that no work can contribute to salvation (cf. Rom. 3:20, 27-28; 4:2-5). Repentance here is "right-about face, a change of mind and attitude instead of a complacent self-satisfaction and pride of race and privilege" (A. T. Robertson).

2 Corinthians 7:9, 10

In this passage, Paul says that he was comforted by the coming of Titus with a message about the Corinthians (2 Cor. 7:6). He adds that Titus told him about their "earnest desire," their "mourning" and their "zeal" for Paul (2 Cor 7:7). The Corinthians desired to see Paul again, but they mourned over having not disciplined the disobedient brother (1 Cor. 5:2) and having caused Paul grief. They were still zealous for Paul over against those who were attacking him. Upon hearing this good report from Titus, Paul rejoiced (2 Cor. 7:7).

Paul explains his comfort and joy. "For even if I made you sorry with my letter, I do not regret it; though I did regret it. For I perceive that the same epistle made you sorry, though only for a while. Now I rejoice, not that you were made sorry, but that your sorrow led to repentance. For you were made sorry in a godly manner, that you might suffer loss from us in nothing" (2 Cor. 7:8-9). His explanation sounds complicated, but it is rather simple.

A man in the church at Corinthian was living in sexual immorality and the church did nothing about it (1 Cor. 5:1-13). In 1 Corinthians, Paul rebuked the congregation for its negligence in not dealing with the situation. His rebuke made them sorry, that is, caused them grief and pain (2 Cor. 7:8).

Paul first says that he did not regret having written that letter and then says that he did (2 Cor. 7:8). Paul did not regret what he said, because, as he explains in verse nine, it made them repent. On the other hand, he regretted writing it when he perceived that it made them sorry. Love regrets causing pain even when the pain is necessary as when a parent has to punish a child.

So, Paul says that he is not sorry that he made them sorrow, because their sorrow led them to repent. The statement that their "sorrow led to repentance" clearly demonstrates that there is a difference between sorrow and repentance. Their sorrow was that they had disappointed Paul. It led them to repent, that is, change their minds about dealing with the adultery in their midst.

Having said they were sorry in a godly manner, Paul now explains two kinds of sorrow: "For godly sorrow produces repentance leading to salvation, not to be regretted, but the sorrow of the world produces death" (2 Cor. 7:10). Godly sorrow takes God's will into account. It produces a change of mind that leads "to salvation." The Greek word rendered "salvation" means "deliverance." It is a flexible term which can refer to deliverance from sickness, difficulties, physical death and condemnation (Lk. 3:48; Acts 27:31; 2 Cor. 1:6; Eph. 2:8-9; Phil. 1:19). In this case it refers to deliverance from God's discipline (Wilkin, dissertation, p. 129). Such sorrow is never to be regretted either by the person who causes it or the person who experiences it.

On the other hand, a sorrow for doing something wrong that leaves God out of the account is merely remorse, "that melancholy compound of self-pity and self-disgust." It has no healing power (Tasker). "World grief does not progress beyond remorse" (Kruse). It produces death, not life. Thus, there is not a change of mind that leads to God and deliverance.

2 Corinthians 12:21

Having said that he wrote for their edification (2 Cor. 12:19), Paul goes on to say, "For I fear, lest when I come, I shall not find you such as I wish, and that I shall be found by you such as you do not wish; lest there be contentions, jealousies, outbursts of wrath, selfish ambitions, backbiting, whisperings, conceits, tumults" (2 Cor. 12:20).

Paul was afraid that when he came, the Corinthians would not be where he wanted them to be spiritually, that is, they would be carnal practicing sins such as contentions, etc. If that happened, he would not be what they wanted him to be, that is, gentle (1 Cor. 4:21).

If Paul arrived in Corinth and some of them were practicing these sins, he would be deeply grieved. Thus, he adds, "And lest, when I come again, my God will humble me among you, and I shall mourn for many who have sinned before and have not repented of the uncleanness, fornication and licentiousness which they have practiced" (2 Cor. 12:21).

If such sins were present when he came, then instead of coming in joy (cf. 2 Cor. 3:2), he would be coming in sorrow (cf. 2 Cor. 2:1-3). Even though in such a case he would say God used it to humble him, he didn't want the humbling experience of lamenting unrepentant sin.

This passage poses several questions. Is Paul speaking about genuine believers? What is the meaning of his use of the word "repent"?

Some argue that the sins listed here were only being committed by a "minority" and it demonstrates that the people about whom Paul is speaking were not genuine believers (Hughes), but Paul speaks of "many who have sinned" (2 Cor. 12:21) and in light of what he says about this church (cf. 1 Cor. 1:2, 4-7; 6:18-20; 12:13; 2 Cor.1:8; 6:14-7:1) it is hard to imagine that Paul considered "many" in the church to be unregenerate

(Wilkin, dissertation, p. 131). These were believers who had continued to practice immorality "even after their conversion" (Tasker; see also Hodge). When we find a believer committing serious sin, the response should be grief, not criticism, condemnation, anger, or indifference.

What does Paul mean by "repent" in this passage? In light of Paul's use of "repent" earlier in this book (2 Cor. 7:9-10), it is reasonable to assume that the meaning of "repent" here is the same as there, namely, "to change one's mind." In other words, Paul was afraid that they had not changed their attitudes toward the sins he lists (Wilkin, dissertation, p. 130-131).

The list of sins in verse 20, coupled with the ones in verse 21, is virtually a summary of the sins Paul dealt with in 1 Corinthians. The Corinthians had been guilty of contentions and jealousies. Those same sins using the same Greek words are mentioned in 1 Corinthians 3:3 and here. Though not mentioned by name they no doubt had also been guilty of outbursts of anger, self-seeking, evil speaking openly and behind one another's backs ("backbiting" is speaking evil openly and "whisperings" is secret slander), pride (cf. 1 Cor. 4:6, 18, 19; 5:2; 8:1; 13:4), as well as disorder in their divisions and difficulties with each other.

Uncleanness can refer to any impurity, but it is often linked to sexual sins in the New Testament. Fornication is any unlawful sexual activity including adultery and homosexuality. It is at least one form of uncleanness. Licentiousness is excessive sin that is defiant of public decency. The Corinthians had been guilty of all of these kinds of sin (cf. 1 Cor. 5:1; 6:12-20; 11:21). Though some deny that Christians are capable of such sins, this passage indicates that believers can commit all kinds of iniquity. Though conversion itself is instantaneous, growth in grace is gradual.

2 Timothy 2:25

Paul wrote to Timothy, "A servant of the Lord must not quarrel but be gentle to all, able to teach, patient, in humility correcting those who are in opposition, if God perhaps will grant them repentance, so that they may know the truth, and that they may come to their senses and escape the snare of the devil, having been taken captive by him to do his will" (2 Tim. 2:24-26). These verses also provoke several critical questions.

Are the members of the opposition believers or unbelievers? Several factors indicate that they are believers. The Greek word rendered "correcting," means "to child train, to teach, to correct." Child training, correcting, is for believers, not unbelievers. Furthermore, the Greek word translated "come to their senses" means "to return to soberness." Returning implies that these are "true believers" (Kent). People cannot return to something, in this case a doctrine (see next paragraph), unless they previously held to it. Hence, "Paul has in mind the constructive re-education of misguided Christian brethren" (J. N. D. Kelly).

TRUTH ⊂ B.P.

What were they opposing? Apparently, they were opposing the truth, because Paul says they need to "know the truth." The issue in this passage is straying from the truth (2 Tim. 2:18). Hymenaeus and Philetus did that by "saying that the resurrection is already past" (2 Tim. 2:17-18). Paul warns Timothy to "be diligent to present yourself approved to God, a worker who does not need to be ashamed, rightly dividing the word of truth" (2 Tim 2:15). In other words, even Timothy must be careful, so that he will not stray from the truth.

Is it possible for a believer to deny the resurrection? Some in the congregation at Corinth either doubted or denied the idea of a resurrection from the dead, or perhaps, more specifically, just the resurrection of believers. Paul says, "Now if Christ is preached that He has been raised from the dead, how do some among you say that there no resurrection of the dead?" (1 Cor. 15:12). Some within the congregation (cf. "among you") were doubting or denying (cf. "say") the resurrection of the dead. They were asking such questions as, "How are the dead raised up?" and "With what body do they come." Paul begins a long defense of the resurrection (that is, all of 1 Cor. 15) by declaring that all Christians believe Christ was raised because that is what they had to believe in order to be converted (1 Cor. 15:1-11). Evidently, some believed in the resurrection of Christ, but were doubting or denying the resurrection of believers.

What does Paul mean by God granting repentance? It means that God gives people the opportunity to repent" (See comments on Acts 5:31).

What does Paul mean by repentance? Timothy is to correct these believers so they will repent, know the truth, and come to their senses. Therefore, in this passage, the word "repent" means to "change one's mind." The result of repenting is they will come to their senses and will know the truth. Simply put, repentance here is a "change of mind to come to a recognition of truth" (Guthrie). It is a "change of attitude enabling them to arrive at an acknowledgement of the truth" (J. N. D. Kelly).

(No – Learn Bib. Doc.

Summary: Paul's message of repentance to unbelievers was that they should change their minds about idols and trust Jesus Christ. People must give up attitudes that prevent them from trusting Jesus Christ. His message of repentance to believers was that they should change their minds about tolerating or practicing sin. Believers are to change their minds from believing sin is permissible to believing that it is not permissible.

Wilkin says that there are approximately thirty-four references in Paul's epistles giving a condition(s) of salvation (see Wilkin, dissertation, p. 120 for the list of reference). Of these, thirty-two condition salvation on faith alone and two on repentance alone (one of the two does not mention the word). In other words, there is a "notable lack of emphasis" on repentance as a requirement for salvation in Paul's epistles (Wilkin, dissertation, p. 118). Wilkin quotes others who say that in Paul's writings repentance plays a negligible role (Bultmann) or Paul almost totally neglected and ignored repentance as a condition of salvation (Andrews).

If repentance is required for the forgiveness of sins, what is the explanation of Paul's lack of emphasis on repentance? That is not a problem, provided that it is understood that while repentance and faith can be distinguished, they are inseparable. New Testament faith is changing one's mind from believing one thing to believing another. In the case of salvation, it is changing one's mind from trusting one's own righteousness, or an idol to trusting Jesus Christ. For believers, it is changing one's mind from believing that sin does not matter to believing what God says about it. Everyone needs to repent, that is, all need to believe God!

Belief is not part of repent.

Chapter 7

THE MESSAGE IN THE BOOK OF HEBREWS

The word "repentance" appears in the book of Hebrews three times. In one of these passages it is connected to faith and in the other two it occurs alone.

Hebrews Six

Hebrews 6:1

The original recipients of the book of Hebrews were spiritually immature believers (Heb. 5:11-14). The author exhorts them to go on to maturity (Heb. 6:1). In the process of doing that, the author tells them: "Therefore, leaving the discussion of the elementary principles of Christ, let us go on to perfection, not laying again the foundation of repentance from dead works and of faith toward God" (Heb. 6:1).

Repentance from dead works is a change of mind about the rituals of the Mosaic Law. The expression "dead works" occurs here and in Hebrews 9:14 where it is said to be Levitical rituals (Hodges). Dead works are works that have no life. They lack "any effective power for obtaining justification" (Guthrie). All efforts to please God are "merely dead works" and the only hope of salvation is a complete reversal of attitude. The sinner "must cease trusting his own righteousness (which is no righteousness at all) and must cast himself upon the mercy of God, receiving by faith the gift of salvation" (Kent). What is needed is faith directed toward God. Ironside puts it like this:

> What then is meant by "repentance from dead works"? It is a complete change of mind, whereby the convicted sinner gives up all thought of being able to propitiate God by effort of his own and acknowledges that he is as bad as the Word has declared him to be. He turns right about face. Instead of relying on his own fancied merits he turns to the Lord for deliverance and seeks for mercy through the Savior God has provided (Ironside, p. 83).

> "Repentance from dead works," then implies the giving up of all confidence in the flesh, the recognition that I am not able to do one thing to retrieve my fallen estate. As a dead sinner I cannot do one thing to merit the divine favor. My prayers, my tears, my charity, my religiousness, all count for nothing, so far as earning salvation is concerned. I am lost and need a Savior. I am sick and need a Physician. I am bankrupt and need a Kinsman-Redeemer. I am dead and need Him who is the Resurrection and the Life. All I need I find in Christ, for whom I count all else but dross (Ironside, pp. 89-90).

This reference again demonstrates that nature of repentance is not sorrow for sin or changing one's behavior. It is not saying people have to feel sorrow for their works or stop doing one kind of works and start doing another kind of works. It is saying that people need to change their minds about their works. If people are depending on their works, which of course are dead since works have no life or ability to save, and they change their minds about works being able to save, they will then need to trust something or someone else. As the next phrase indicates that someone else is Jesus Christ.

This is the third time in the New Testament where repentance and faith are mentioned together (cf. Mk. 1:15; Acts 20:21). In this case the two are linked together. People are to change their minds about trusting their works for forgiveness and trust Jesus Christ.

Repentance and faith are foundational. The author is saying that the readers need to press on beyond foundational truth to more advanced thinking, which will lead to maturity.

Hebrews 6:6

The author explains they should go on to maturity. "For it is impossible for those who were once enlightened, and have tasted the heavenly gift and have become partakers of the Holy Spirit, and have tasted the good Word of God and the powers of the age to come, if they fall away, to renew them again to repentance, since they crucify again for themselves the Son of God and put Him to open shame" (Heb. 6:4-6).

These verses constitute a single sentence. Simply put it says, "It is impossible for those who were enlightened to be renewed again to repentance." Actually, four participle phrases (literally translated: having been enlightened . . . having tasted . . . having become partakers . . . having tasted) describe the people involved. The greatly debated question is who are these individuals? Are they genuinely regenerated? _ They are!

John Calvin and many others say, "No." According to that view these people were enlightened, that is, exposed to the gospel or even illuminated, but not regenerate. They tasted, but they did not drink. They were partakers of the work of the Holy Spirit, but not the person of the Holy Spirit (Calvin; Newell; Lenski; Bruce).

A careful consideration of the content of these verses in the context of Hebrews, however, indicates that genuinely regenerate individuals are being described. The Greek word translated "enlightened" here is only used in one other place in Hebrews, namely, in Hebrews 10:32, where it definitely describes true believers (Kent). To be enlightened is to be converted (2 Cor 4:3-6; Hodges). The addition of "once" to enlightened "marks the completeness and sufficiency of the single act" (Westcott). It points to "something complete, rather than partial or inadequate" (Kent).

Likewise the Greek word rendered "tasted" is used elsewhere in Hebrews of actual experience (cf. 2:9; see also 1 Pet. 2:3). In the illustration that follows, the land "drinks" the rain, a heavenly gift (Heb. 6:7). To taste of the heavenly gift, then, is to experience the gift of eternal life (Jn. 4:10; Rom. 6:23; Jas. 1:17-18; Westcott; Hodges).

The Greek word for "partakers" is also used elsewhere in Hebrews of regenerate people. In Hebrews 3:1 it is used of partaking of the heavenly calling and in Hebrews 3:14 of being partakers of Christ! To partake of the Holy Spirit is to participate with the person of the Holy Spirit (Westcott, Kent).

In the Greek text as well as the English, the word "tasted" is used twice. They not only experienced the gift of eternal life (Heb. 6:4) they also experienced the goodness of the Word of God and the powers of the age to come (Heb. 6:5). The word translated "powers" is the normal New Testament word for miracles. They had witnessed miracles, the power of God in the present that will also be manifest in the age to come (cf. Heb. 2:4; Kent; Hodges).

Thus, there is no question but that the individuals referred to in Hebrews 6:4-5 are genuinely regenerate. The context (Heb. 5:11-6:3) and the content of these verses support such a conclusion. In the words of another, "the normal understanding of these descriptive terms, in light of the author's own use elsewhere in the epistle, is to those who are regenerate" (Kent).

The next question concerns the falling away. In the English text verse 6 reads "if they fall away," but in the Greek text "fall away" is a participle like the four descriptive phrases of Hebrews 6:4-5. A more accurate translation would be, "It is impossible for those who having been once enlightened and having tasted the heavenly gift and having become partakers of the Holy Spirit and having tasted the good Word of God and the powers of the age to come and having fallen away to be renewed again to repentance." The Greek verb "fall away" occurs only here in the New Testament, although the noun occurs much more than that (cf. for example, Gal. 6:1). The idea is of falling aside from the right path (Westcott) and here refers to deliberate apostasy (Heb. 3:12; Bruce; Guthrie), that is, defection from the faith, withdrawal from a Christian profession (Hodges).

Is it possible for a genuine regenerate person to deny the faith? Apparently. Consider the fact that John warns believers (1

Jn. 2:12-14) that false teachers were trying to deceive them (1 Jn. 2:26) concerning the doctrine of Christ (1 Jn. 2:21-25). Paul said something similar. (2 Cor. 11:1-4, 13-15; see also 2 Tim 2:17-18).

In other words, this passage is saying that it is impossible for a regenerate person to apostatize and be renewed again to repentance. The Greek word rendered "renew" only occurs here in the New Testament and means "to restore." In the Greek text, it is in the active voice and Westcott argues that "the use of the active voice limits the strict application of the words to human agency" and that the fact that it is also in the present tense "suggests continual effort." It is impossible for continuous effort on the part of people to restore an apostate back, not to conversion but to commitment (Hodges).

What then is the meaning of the word "repentance" in Hebrews 6:6? Some interpret Hebrews 6 as hypothetical (Westcott). If that is the case, the word "repentance" is identical to Hebrews 6:1 and means that it is impossible for a genuine believers to repent again (change their minds about good works), which is another way of saying be saved again. The point would be to go on to maturity because you cannot be saved again.

Others say that this is not hypothetical (Hodges). It is really impossible for genuine believers who return to a works system of salvation (such as Judaism) to have their minds changed either by God (Kent) or by man (Hodges).

Either way (hypothetical or actual) the meaning of the word "repentance" in verse 6 is "change your mind."

Hebrews Twelve

In Hebrews 12, the author warns believers not to fall short of the grace of God, lest a root of bitterness spring up (Heb. 12:15) or lest there be a fornicator or profane person, that is, one who is "worldly irreligious" (Heb. 12:16). Esau is given as an illustration of a profane person.

Esau sold his birthright for a bowl of lentil soup (Gen. 25:29-34). The birthright was the right of the oldest son to be the head of the family. Under the Mosaic Law the eldest son received a double inheritance (Deut. 21:17). Esau valued things earthly and present more than he did things heavenly and future (Lang). For a temporary gratification, he forfeited his inheritance (Hodges). He put the sensual above the spiritual. He was a worldly, irreligious person.

That does not mean Esau was not a believer. He was a son who was entitled to an inheritance (Lang). He lost his inheritance, not his sonship. Nor does it mean he had no spiritual interest at all. In fact, the author says, "For you know that afterward, when he wanted to inherit the blessing, he was rejected, for he found no place for repentance, though he sought it diligently with tears" (Heb. 12:17). In other words, Esau later wanted to inherit the blessing; he changed his mind and even was moved to tears over his foolishness, but it was too late (Gen 27:34-35). He could not reverse what he had done (Guthrie); he could not reverse the consequences of his former decision (Wilkin, *JOTGES*, Autumn, 1990, p. 29).

Summary: Repentance in the book of Hebrews is a change of mind. It is used of a change of mind about dead works (Heb. 6:1, 6) and a change of mind about a previous decision (Heb. 12:17).

Repentance in Hebrews is changing one's mind from believing in dead works to believing in Christ, or in Esau's case, changing one's mind from believing soup was more important than inheritance to believing that inheritance is more important than soup.

Chapter 8

THE MESSAGE OF JOHN THE APOSTLE

J ohn was present when Jesus told the Apostles to preach repentance to all nations (Lk. 24:47). Unlike Peter and Paul, John's sermons are not recorded in the books of Acts. He did, however, write five books of the New Testament. In four of those books, John does not use the words "repent" or "repentance" at all. The verb "repent" appears in the fifth book, the book of Revelation, twelve times. In terms of a study of repentance in the New Testament it is important to look at two of John's five books.

The Gospel of John

The Gospel of John is the only book in the Bible that states that its purpose is to convert its readers. John the Apostle writes, "And truly Jesus did many other signs in the presence of His disciples, which are not written in this book; but these are written that you may believe that Jesus is the Christ, the Son of God, and that believing you may have life in His name" (Jn. 20:30-31). Therefore, it is surprising to discover that the words "repent" and "repentance" do not make an appearance in the book at all, not one single time. In twenty-one chapters of evangelistic material there is not so much as one reference to repentance.

In fact, the Apostle seems to deliberately avoid the word "repent." He gives more attendance to the ministry of John the Baptist than the synoptic Gospels, each of which summarize John's ministry by reporting that he preached "repent" [Wilkin says the Gospel of John contains 29 verses concerning the preaching of John the Baptist (Jn. 1:6-8, 19-36; 3:23-30) as compared to 15 in Matthew (Mt. 3:1-15), 10 in Mark (Mk. 1:2-11) and 19 in Luke (Lk. 3:2-20), Wilkin, dissertation, pp. 154-155]. Nevertheless, in the Gospel of John, the Apostle never mentions the word, even in connection with the ministry of John the Baptist.

The Gospel of John never mentions John the Baptist's denunciation of the self-righteous attitude of the Jews who thought that being of Abraham's descent gained them a place in the world to come (Mt. 3:9; Lk. 3:8). It does not call the baptism of John the baptism of repentance (Mt. 3:11; Mk. 1:4; Lk. 3:3). It does not report that John the Baptist called for fruit fitting repentance (Mt. 3:8; Lk. 3:8). All of these observations would have been appropriate when speaking of the preaching of John the Baptist. Matthew, Mark and Luke certainly thought so, but the Gospel of John, the only Biblical book with an evangelistic purpose, omits all such references to repentance.

At one point in the Gospel of John, the author records a dialogue between John the Baptist and a delegation from Jerusalem. They ask, "Who are you?" (Jn. 1:19). John denies that he is the Christ, Elijah, or the Prophet and identifies himself as a voice of one crying in the wilderness (Jn. 1:20-24). The delegation then asks, "Why then do you baptize if you are not the Christ, nor Elijah, nor the Prophet?" (Jn. 1:25). According to Matthew, Mark and Luke, John the Baptist preached a "baptism of repentance" (Mt. 3:11; Mk. 1:4; Lk. 3:3). So, it would be expected that the Gospel of John would report that John said his baptism was a baptism of repentance, but it does not do that! Instead, John says, "I baptize with water, but there stands One among you whom you do not know. It is He who, coming after me, is preferred before me, whose sandal strap I am not worthy to loose" (Jn. 1:26-27). This is a place in the Gospel of John where repentance would definitely be expected, but there is nothing, not even a hint, about repentance.

It is not that the author of the fourth Gospel did not know that John the Baptist preached repentance. He did know, because John, the author of the Gospel of John, was once a disciple of John the Baptist.

In the Gospel of John, after the conversation between John the Baptist and the delegation from Jerusalem, the author says, "Again, the next day, John (the Baptist) stood with two of his disciples" (Jn. 1:35). Those two disciples of John the Baptist "followed Jesus" (Jn. 1:37). One of the two is identified as "Andrew, Simon Peter's brother" (Jn. 1:40). The second is not named, but "from early times" it has been thought that he was John, who later wrote the Gospel of John (Morris; so, Westcott; A. T. Robertson; Vincent; F. F. Bruce; et al.). Indeed, "it is difficult to suppose that the other was not the author of the narrative which is to follow" (Godet). If the author of this passage was once a "pupil" of John the Baptist, "his silence on the theme of repentance is made all the more amazing" (Zane Hodges, *Absolutely Free*, p. 148).

On the other hand, the author of the Gospel of John states that the purpose of the ministry of John the Baptist was faith. John says, "There was a man sent from God, whose name was John. This man came for a witness, to bear witness of the Light, that all through him might believe" (Jn. 1:6-7).

While the words for repent and repentance do not occur in the Gospel of John, what it does say is that one must believe in order to have eternal life. If repentance is required for the forgiveness of sins, for John repentance must be included (in) believing. If repentance were required as a separate act from believing, it is inconceivable that John would never have made reference to it (Baker, p. 414).

The Book of Revelation

In seven different passages in the book of Revelation, the Greek verb "repent" appears twelve times. In five of these passages the word is used of believers and in two it is directed to unbelievers.

Revelation 2:5 (twice)

Jesus told the church at Ephesus that they had left their first love (Rev. 2:4). He then counsels them: "Remember therefore from where you have fallen; repent and do the first works, or else I will come to you quickly and remove your lamp stand from its place;

unless you repent" (Rev. 2:5). Jesus gives them three commands: remember, repent and repeat the first works.

The placement of "repent" between "remember" and "do" indicates that repentance in this passage is somewhere between remembering and doing. They were to recall their former love for Christ, change their mind from their current less-than-loving attitude and begin to do again loving deeds. The loving actions were fruit of their change of mind.

Walvoord says that the word repent means "to change the mind" and adds that the Ephesians "were to have a different attitude toward Christ and should resume that fervent love which once they had" (Walvoord, p. 57). *He got it wrong. They were to change their minds from whatever they believed gave them the right to walk out of IHS to getting back in fellowship and walk in Spirit*

Revelation 2:16

Jesus told the church at Pergamos that some of them had fallen into false doctrine (Rev. 2:14), which involved idolatry and associated with it, immorality (Rev. 14-15). Some within the church taught that Christians had the liberty to participate in the pagan temples and its sexual immorality. The sexual immorality mentioned here was part of pagan festivities (Mounce, p. 98).

The backdrop of this may be the demand for emperor worship. As Hadjiantoniou explains it, there were those in the church that reasoned that a few grains of incense have no importance whatever. So, throw a few grains of incense on the altar and a little smoke will go up. It is nothing but smoke. When the others bow their heads, bow yours—your head, not your heart. It is reasonable to believe that your relation to Christ will not be affected by such trivial, external things as a few grains of incense, a puff of smoke, and a slight inclination of the head (Hadjiantoniou, p. 58-59).

Jesus tells the church, "Repent, or else I will come to you quickly and will fight against them with the sword of My mouth" (Rev. 2:16). Like the church at Corinth, the church at Pergamos had failed to discipline its members (see Mounce). The problem was the church (cf. "you") tolerated those holding to false teaching (cf. "them"). They were to change their minds from an attitude of tolerance to an attitude of intolerance toward false teaching in their midst (Wilkin, dissertation, p. 164).

Revelation 2:21 (twice), 2:22

Jesus told the church at Thyatira that they had a similar problem as the church at Pergamos, namely, participating in idolatry and practicing sexual immorality. In this case, it comes from a different source, a prophetess, and their guilt seems to be greater. Concerning the church in Pergamos it was said that they "have" members who hold to the doctrine of Balaam (Rev. 2:14). This time it is said that they "allow" such things to be taught and practiced (Rev. 2:20).

Thyatira was filled with trade guilds. It was difficult, if not impossible, to make a living without belonging to one. The craftsman had to become a member of a guild. The problem for a believer was that belonging to a trade guild meant attending its meals, which were often held in pagan temples. Even if the meal was not in a temple, it began and ended with a formal sacrifice to the gods, and the meat eaten would be meat which had already been offered to idols. The meal also degenerated into sexual immorality. — *Part of pagan festival sex god*

A prophetess called Jezebel, which was probably not her real name (what Jewish couple would name their daughter *or god* Jezebel?), no doubt, claimed divine revelation for her teaching *she was* that it was permissible to participate in such practices. Perhaps *was a* the church allowed her to teach in the name of unity. *gentile*

As hideous as her sin was, the Lord first dealt with her graciously. He says, "I gave her time to repent of her sexual immorality, and she did not repent" (Rev. 2:21). Instead of telling the church to repent as He did the church at Pergamos, the Lord speaks of the guilty individuals repenting. The Greek word translated "repent" means "to change one's mind" and it "has its literal significance here" (Smith).

She did not change her mind concerning what she was teaching (Rev. 2:20) and doing (Rev. 2:21). Since she did not respond to God's grace and patience, He will deal with her and her followers in judgment. He says, "Indeed I will cast her into a sickbed, and those who commit adultery with her into *her children* great tribulation, unless they repent of their deeds. I will kill *are* her children with death" (Rev. 2:22-23). He will judge her with *followers* sickness. There is a contrast between the bed of her pleasure and this bed of her punishment. Paul taught that God uses sickness

Religious adultery, same as Israel (No.) in 8th Cent and Judah (So.) in 7th & 6th Cent.

This adultery is against God by His children, by them going to the pagan/false religion.

to disciple believers (1 Cor. 11:29-30). Her bed of sin would become a bed of sickness.

He will judge those who commit adultery with her with great tribulation, unless they repent. These are probably believers who accepted her teaching and consequently committed adultery (cf. "my servants" in verse 20). The Greek word for "tribulation" means, "pressure, tribulation, affliction, distress." Their affliction will be great.

He will judge her children with death. Her children are not her literal offspring, but her followers. It is also possible that these are those, who, like her, taught what she taught.

Revelation 3:3

Temporal Death

Jesus told the church at Sardis that as a whole it was dead (Rev. 3:2). From a Biblical point of view, it is possible to be living and dead at the same time. Paul speaks of a widow, who is assumed to be a believer but "who lives in pleasure." He says that she is "dead while she lives" (1 Tim. 5:6). The church had some work, but no vital spiritual life.

Based on their spiritual condition, the Lord says, "Be watchful and strengthen the things which remain, that are ready to die, for I have not found your works perfect before God. Remember therefore how you have received and heard; hold fast and repent" (Rev. 3:2-3). Those who were about to die but had a little life are told to "be watchful and strengthen." These are believers; they had heard and received the Word.

These believers are told to be watchful, strengthen what remains, remember what they had heard and received, hold it fast and repent. They had responded correctly at first. They needed to remember that, hold fast to it and repent; that is, *mind* change their attitude back to what it was then. The benefits of reflecting on one's first experience of salvation are repeatedly recognized in the New Testament (cf. Col. 2:6; Heb. 3:14; 10:32; Gal. 5:7).

Revelation 3:19

Jesus rebuked the church at Laodicea for their self-satisfied attitude about their spiritual condition. Nevertheless, they were believers. This letter is addressed to a church (Rev. 3:14). Spewing them out of His mouth (Rev. 3:16) does not mean that they were lost, only that their works indicated that they were lukewarm (Rev. 3:15) and therefore, they made the Lord nauseous. He tells them that they are wretched, miserable, poor, blind, and naked (Rev. 3:17), but believers can be all of those things, including being deceived about their spiritual condition (Jas. 1:22), poor (1 Tim. 6:18), and blind (2 Pet. 1:9). Furthermore, the Lord tells them that He will chasten them, a Greek word that refers to child training, an activity of God to believers (Heb. 12:5-8, esp. 12:8).

The Lord tells these self-satisfied believers to "repent" (Rev. 3:19), which means that they needed to change their opinion concerning their spiritual condition.

Revelation 9:20-21

After a third of the population of the earth is killed (Rev. 9:15), "the rest of mankind, who were not killed by these plagues, did not repent of the works of their hands, that they should not worship demons, and idols of gold, silver, brass, stone, and wood, which can neither see nor hear nor walk. And they did not repent of their murders or their sorceries or their sexual immorality or their thefts" (Rev. 9:20-21). They will worship demons and idols (Deut. 32:17; 1 Cor. 10:20) and as a result, they will commit murder, sorceries and sexuality immorality. They were so hardened, that they "would not change their minds" (Smith).

In the book of Acts, Paul preached that people needed to repent concerning idols, that is, change their minds about the nature of God (Acts 17:30). In Revelation 9, John uses the word "repent" of people changing their minds about idols and adds that they should also change their minds about the immorality that is associated with idolatry. *Say cults*

Revelation 16:9, 11

After the judgment of the fourth bowl, "men were scorched with great heat, and they blasphemed the name of God who has power over these plagues; and they did not repent and give Him glory" (Rev. 16:9). After the judgment of the fifth bowl "they blasphemed the God of heaven because of their pains and their sores, and did not repent of their deeds" (Rev. 16:11).

The repentance in this passage plainly has to do with changing one's mind about God. The Greek text reads *the* men (Rev. 16:9), indicating that the ones scorched are the ones who received the mark and worshiped the Antichrist (Rev. 16:2). These judgments are on the image worshipers (Smith). Moreover, verse nine says they "blasphemed the name of God" and did not "give Him glory." Verse 11 mentions "their deeds," but does not identify them. In the context the deeds must refer to idolatry (Rev. 16:2, 9). They will blaspheme God "instead of crying out to Him for mercy (Wilkin, dissertation, p. 171). The bowl judgments should have resulted in people's "humble confession of dependence on God" (Ladd, cited by Wilkin, dissertation, p. 171). Again, John is using the word "repent" like Paul did in Acts 17:30.

The author of the book of Revelation certainly was not saying people had to turn from their sin in order to be saved, because if that is what he meant he would be repudiating everything he said in the Gospel of John and what he said at the end of this book. He concluded this volume with these words, "And the Spirit and the bride say, 'Come!' And let him who hears say, 'Come!' And let him who thirsts come. Whoever desires, let him take the water of life freely" (Rev 22:17). The Greek word translated "freely" means "without cost." John would not say that people had to do something in order to be saved and in the same book say that it is without cost. He would say, however, that people had to change their minds from believing in idols and the sins of idol worship to trusting Jesus Christ.

Summary: In the book of Revelation, the Apostle John uses the word "repent" to describe the message of Jesus to the churches and to delineate what sinners must do in the Tribulation. In both cases, it involves a change of one's mind.

And in the Church Chps 2-3

CONCLUSION

Repent is the most misunderstood word in the Bible. Definitions include, changing one's mind, feeling sorrow for sin, ceasing to sin, and even doing acts of penance. Then, there is the problem of the relation of repentance to faith. Does repentance come before, with or after faith? No wonder there is so much confusion.

In the New Testament, the Greek words "repent" and "repentance" mean "to change one's mind." The object of what people are changing their minds about is determined by the context. The message of repentance is preached to unbelievers and believers.

To Unbelievers

When John the Baptist preached "repent," he meant change your mind about trusting your merit to enter the world to come and trust the Christ who is about to come.

When Jesus proclaimed "repent," He meant change your mind from trusting yourself that you are righteous to trusting God's mercy (Lk. 18:9-14) or change your mind concerning who He is.

When Peter urged people to "repent," he meant change your mind about Christ from thinking of Him as a common criminal to Him being the Messiah, the One to trust for the forgiveness of sins.

When Paul admonished people to "repent," he meant change your mind from trusting an idol to trusting Jesus Christ.

When John the Apostle wrote "repent," he meant change your mind from trusting idols with the attending immorality to trusting the true God, Jesus Christ.

The message of repentance to unbelievers was that they had to change their minds. Depending on their mindset, they needed a shift in thinking about their merit to enter the coming kingdom, their righteousness, their works, the nature of God, and who Jesus Christ is. In other words, repentance is changing one's mind from trusting one's merit, righteousness, works, or idols to trusting Jesus Christ. Repentance, then, if not equivalent to faith in Christ, is conceptually equivalent to faith or essentially synonymous with faith.

Chafer has written that repentance "is included in believing and could not be separated from it" (Chafer, vol. 3, p. 373). "Repentance, which is a change of mind, is included in believing. No individual can turn to Christ from some other confidence without a change of mind" (Chafer, vol. 3, p. 374). There are passages where the word repentance is a "synonym of believing" (Chafer, vol. 3, p. 377). He concludes that repentance, which is a change of mind, is a necessity to enter into the very act of believing in Christ, "since one cannot turn to Christ from other objects of confidence without that change of mind" (Chafer, vol. 3, p. 378).

Ironside says, "So intimately are the two related that you cannot have one without the other. The man who believes God repents; the repentant soul puts his trust in the Lord when the Gospel is revealed to him" (Ironside, p. 16).

In his sermon entitled "Faith and Repentance Inseparable," Charles Haddon Spurgeon says, "No repentance is worth the having which is not perfectly consistent with faith in Christ."

As Ironside says, "Everywhere the apostles went they called upon men thus to face their sins—to face the question of their helplessness, yet their responsibility to God—to face Christ as the one, all sufficient Savior, and thus by trusting him to obtain the remission of sins and justification from all things. So to face these tremendous facts is to change one's mind completely" (Ironside, p. 15).

From a Biblical point of view, the repentance that is required for salvation includes faith and the faith that is required includes repentance.

To Believers

When Jesus said that a brother needed to repent, He meant that he needed to change his mind about sinning against another brother. When Peter used the word "repent" in speaking to a believer, he meant that he needed to change his mind about buying the ability to bestow the Holy Spirit by the laying on of hands. When Paul used the word "repent" in speaking to believers, he meant that they needed to change their minds concerning their toleration of sin. When John used the word "repent" in speaking to believers, he also meant that they needed to change their minds concerning their tolerance of sin.

Ironside observed that since saints are sinners, there is "the need of daily and constant self-judgment which, we have seen, is the true meaning of sincere repentance" (Ironside, p. 69). He quotes a believer who said, "I repented before I knew the meaning of the word. I have repented far more since, than I did then" (Ironside, p. 11).

Summary: Repentance is changing one's mind from believing one thing to believing another.

Repentance is connected with faith, even in a non-religious case in the Old Testament. Proverbs says, "The simple believes every word, but the prudent considers well his steps" (Prov. 14:15). In the Septuagint, the Greek translation of the Old Testament, the word translated "considers well" is translated by the Greek word for repent. Hence, in this proverb, the simple *believe* everything they hear, but the prudent don't believe; they consider well what they do, meaning that in contrast to the simple, they change their minds from what they hear then they believe. Notice the connection between belief and repentance in this proverb!

There are places in the New Testament where repentance is a virtual synonym for faith. Jesus said that the men of Nineveh repented at the preaching of Jonah (Mt. 12:41); the book of Jonah says that the people of Nineveh believed God (Jonah 3:5). Peter told the people in Cornelius's house that "whoever believes in Him will receive remission of sins" (Acts 10:43), but when Peter got back to Jerusalem, he said that "God gave them the same gift as *He gave* us when we believed on the Lord Jesus Christ" (Acts 11:17) and the people in Jerusalem said, 'Then God has also granted to the Gentiles repentance to life'" (Acts 11:18). What has been described as faith (Acts 10:43; 11:17) is now called repentance (Acts 11:18). Paul declared to the people of Athens that God "commands all men everywhere to repent" (Acts 17:29-30), but the episode ends with Luke saying that some "believed" (Acts 17:34).

Synech

If this is the way that God's Word uses "repent," how can anyone do otherwise? Those who use the term in any other way need to repent; they need to change their minds.

Appendix 1

A WORD STUDY ON REPENTANCE

Word studies of Biblical words trace the various meaning of a word throughout history. Thus, a word study of a New Testament word includes: (1) the root meaning of the word; (2) its classical usage, which means how it was used between 900-300 B.C.; (3) its usage in the Koine period (300 B.C.-100 A.D.); that is, how it was used in the common, every day world outside the New Testament; (4) its usage in the Septuagint, the Greek translation of the Old Testament (ca. 250 B.C.); and (5) its usage in the New Testament.

Needless to say, the critical issue is not the root meaning, or the meaning of a word at another time or in another place, but how a word is used in the New Testament in the context in which it appears. With that in mind, here is a brief word study of the New Testament Greek words "repent" (a verb) and "repentance" (a noun).

The Root Meaning

The Greek word for repentance (*metanoia*) is made up of the two words: "after" (*meta*) and "mind" (*noia*). The root meaning of the word "repentance" then, is "afterthought, change of mind."

Classical Usage

One of the recognized authorities on the meanings of Greek words in the Classical period is the *Greek-English Lexicon*, by Liddell and Scott. It says that the meaning of "repent" by Plato

(427-347 B.C.) and Xenophon (ca. 434-ca. 355 B.C.) is to "change one's mind or purpose" and that the meaning of "repentance" by Thucydides (ca. 471-ca. 400 B.C.) is "afterthought" (Liddell and Scott, p. 503).

Wilkin gives the specifics. Claiming that in Classical Greek, "repentance" means "changing one's mind," he cites Thucydides, who when writing about the response of the Athenian council to a revolt decided that not just those who participated in the revolt, but all the men of the city of Meytilene were to be put to death. On the next day, however, they repented, that is, changed their minds. They decided that only the participants were to be put to death. He then quotes Xenophon, who said, "We were inclined to conclude that for man, as he is constituted, it is easier to rule over any and all other creatures than to rule over men. But when we reflected that there was one Cyrus, the Persian, who reduced to obedience a vast number of men and cities and nations, we were then compelled to change our opinions (repent) and decide that to rule men might be a task neither impossible nor even difficult, if one should only go about it in an intelligent manner" (Wilkin, *JOTGES*, Autumn, 1989, pp. 13-14).

Koine Period

The book that gives the meaning of Greek words in papyri documents is *The Vocabulary of the Greek Testament* by Moulton and Milligan. It cites a use of the verb "repent" that means "change of mind" (Moulton and Milligan, p. 404).

Again Wilkin gives the specifics. He cites Polybius (ca. 208-126 B.C.), who used the word "repentance" to describe what the Dardani did. They decided to attack Macedonia while Philip was away. When Philip quickly returned, they changed their minds and broke off the attack before it even began. He also quotes Plutarch (ca. 46 B.C.-ca. 120 A.D.), who wrote, "Cypselus, the father of Periander . . . when he was a new-born babe, smiled at the men who had been sent to make away with him, and they turned away. And when again they changed their minds (repented), they sought for him and found him not, for he had been put away in a chest by his mother" (Wilkin, *JOTGES*, Autumn, 1989, p. 14).

The conclusion given in the *Theological Dictionary of the New Testament* (Kittel) is that for the Greek philosophers *metanoia* was predominantly used "in the intellectual sense. . . . by a penitent alteration of judgment, by reconsideration, for example, by the correction of a mistaken view, the fool becoming a wise man" (Kittel, vol. 4, p. 980). "For the Greeks *metanoia* never suggests an alteration in the total moral attitude, a profound change in life's direction, a conversion which affects the whole of conduct" (Kittel, vol. 4, p. 979).

By the way, assuming that repentance in the New Testament means "to turn from sin," the article in *Theological Dictionary of the New Testament* says, "Whether linguistically or materially one's searches the Greek world in vain for the origin of the New Testament understanding of *metanoeō* and *metanoia*" (Kittel, vol. 4, p. 980). No wonder! The assumption is wrong. Actually, as will be seen from a study of the words "repent" and "repentance" in the New Testament, the facts are that the Greek usage of those words are the same as in the New Testament.

Septuagint

The verb "repent" occurs 19 times in the Septuagint and the noun once (Prov. 14:15). Of these twenty occurrences of "repent" and "repentance," thirteen pertain to God repenting or not repenting (1 Sam. 15:29-twice; Jer. 4:28; 18:8, 18:10; Joel 2:13, 2:14; Amos 7:3, 7:6; Jonah 3:9, 3:10, 4:2; Zech. 8:14). Four of the references to "repent" or "repentance" in the Septuagint are in the book of Proverbs. All four concern people thinking or changing their minds about something (Prov. 14:15; 20:25; 24:32; 29:27 in the LXX; see esp. Prov. 20:25). These are "non-religious" uses of the word. The other three appearances of "repent" are about sinners changing their minds about the nature of God (Isa. 46:8) or their sin (Jer. 8:6; 31:19).

God, of course, does not change His mind. He is omniscient; He knows everything before it happens. To say that God "repents," that is, changes His mind, is an anthropomorphism, a figure of speech attributing a human characteristic to God. When the Scriptures speak of God changing his mind, the change of mind is apparent not actual. Nevertheless, the fact that in the Septuagint God repents demonstrates that repentance is not always about sin. God is not sorry for sin, nor does He turn from sin.

The conclusion is that the Greek words for "repent" and "repentance" in the Septuagint mean "a change of mind."

New Testament

As can be demonstrated, in the New Testament the words "repent" and "repentance" mean "a change of mind." Many passages contain indications in the context that repentance is a change of mind. These include Matthew 3:2 (cf. "do not think" in verse 9 and "fruit worthy of repentance" in verse 8), Matthew 9:13 (cf. "trusted in themselves that they were righteous" in Lk. 18:9), Luke 16:30 (cf. "hear" in verse 29 and "persuade" in verse 31), Acts 8:22 (cf. "thought" in verse 20, "heart" in verse 21 and "the thought of your heart" in verse 22), Acts 17:30 (cf. "not think" in verse 29 and "ignorance" in verse 30), Acts 26:20 (cf. "repent" verses "do works befitting repentance"), 2 Tim. 2:25 (cf. "know" in verse 25 and "come to their senses" in verse 26), Revelation 2:5 (cf. "repent" between "remember" and "do").

Appendix 2

THE HEBREW WORD FOR SORROW

Those who claim that repentance means "to feel remorse" begin with what they say is one of the Old Testament words for repentance. For example, Erickson says that repentance is "based upon a feeling of godly sorrow for the evil we have done" and then says that the Hebrew word that expresses repentance is *nacham*, which means "to lament or to grieve" (Erickson, p. 935).

According to Brown, Driver and Briggs, the Hebrew word *nacham* means "be sorry, console oneself." Other meanings that are listed include "moved to piety, have compassion, suffer grief, repent, be relieved," that is, "ease one's self" by taking vengeance, "comfort, console," etc. (BDB, pp. 636-637).

The Hebrew word *nacham* occurs 108 times in the Old Testament. Sixty-six times it is talking about comfort (for example, cf. Ps. 23:4: "Yea, though I walk through the valley of the shadow of death, I will fear no evil; for You are with me; Your rod and Your staff, they comfort me."). Thirty-six times it is a reference to God repenting. In fact, when it occurs in the sense of "repent," the subject of the verb is almost always "God" rather than "man," a fact that Erickson himself mentions (Erickson, p. 935). Six times it is used of people doing something other than being comforted or comforting.

In other words, according to the Hebrew lexicon, the primary meaning of the Hebrew word *nacham* is "be sorry, console oneself," but English translations usually render it as "comfort" or "repent"; and in the vast majority of times that it means "repent" it is God who is repenting!

Only six times is *nacham* a reference to people doing something other than being comforted or comforting. Of those six, two say that people were "grieved" (Judges 2:6, 15). Of the four remaining, one says people changed their mind (Ex. 13:17) and three say that people repented (Job 42:6; Jer. 8:6; 31:19).

So, in only four passages in the Old Testament (4 out of 108) can it be said that people "repented." In one of those four the point has to do with the children of Israel *changing their minds* about leaving Egypt (Ex. 13:17) and that is the way English translations render it (NKJV; NIV; NAS). In the other three, people are said to repent of their sins.

From this data, several conclusions can be drawn.

1.   There is no technical term for repentance in the Old Testament. Scholars are "generally agreed" that the Old Testament does not have any technical term for repentance (Wilkin, dissertation, pp. 12-13). There is no Hebrew word in the Old Testament which in "all or even in most of its usages refers to repentance" (Wilkin, *JOTGES*, Spring, 1989, p. 14). There is no "special" term in the Old Testament for "repentance" or "to repent" (Würthwein, Kittel, vol. 4, p. 980).

2.   The fact that so many of the references to repentance are about God repenting (36 out of 108) indicate that *nacham* is not feeling sorry for sin, or turning from sin, but can be nothing more than a change of mind.

3.   There are only three references to people repenting (Job 42:6; Jer. 8:6; 31:19). In light of the other references to *nacham*, it is possible and, perhaps, likely that in the Old Testament when *nacham* is used of people repenting it means "a change of mind" (cf. God repenting and see Ex. 13:17). It certainly does not always mean "sorrow." It means the opposite of sorrow, namely "comfort" 66 times out of 108 (see esp. Jer. 31:13).

4.   The three references to people repenting are about believers (in Job 42:6, it is Job; in Jer. 8:6 it is backslidden Israel; cf. Jer. 8:4; in Jer. 31:19 it is returning Israel). Therefore, in none of the three passages in the Old Testament where *nacham* is used of people repenting is the issue gaining eternal life.

5.   Given the scarcity of its use (only three times in all the Old Testament), it is not likely that this rare use of the Hebrew word *nacham* is the background for the word "repent" in the New Testament.

Besides, use, not one possible meaning out of a field of meanings, determines the meaning of a word. The issue, the only issue, is how the word "repent" is used in the New Testament.

Appendix 3

THE HEBREW WORD FOR TURN

Those who say that repentance means "turn from sin" claim that one of the Hebrew words for "repentance" is the Hebrew word *shub* and that it means "to turn." Erickson states that the genuine repentance humans are to display is more commonly designed by this Hebrew word and adds that it stresses the necessity of forsaking sin and entering into fellowship with God (Erickson, p. 936). Behm says that the Greek word for repent "approximates" the Hebrew *shub* (Behm, Kittel, vol. 4, p. 989-90).

Actually, the Hebrew word *shub* means "to turn back, return" (Brown, Driver, and Briggs, p. 996). It occurs 1056 times in the Old Testament, but only about 118 of those are used in a religious sense (Kittel, vol. 4, p. 984; Wilkin counted 203; see dissertation, pp. 210-212 and *JOTGES*, Spring, 1989, p. 15). In the vast majority of cases, it is used to describe a literal change of direction. It is used of God returning to Israel (Josh. 24:20) and of Israel returning to God (Deut. 30:2). In a few instances, it is used of the future turning of Israel and others to the Lord (cf. Isa. 6:10). But in these cases it is another way of speaking about faith, as is indicated by the fact that Isaiah 6:10 is quoted in Acts 28:26-27 to explain why some did not believe (Acts 28:24). (For a more detailed discussion of the Hebrew word *shub* see Wilkin's article in *JOTGES*, Spring, 1989, pp. 15-26.)

The fatal flaw in the assumption that the Hebrew word *shub* is equivalent to the Greek word for repent is that the Greek translation of the Old Testament, the Septuagint, "never" uses *shub* to translate "repent"! In the Septuagint the Greek words that are "always" used for *shub* are *epistrephō* and *apostrephō* (Kittel, vol. 4, p. 989).

BIBLIOGRAPHY

Abbott-Smith, G. *A Manual Greek Lexicon of the New Testament.* Edinburgh: T & T. Clark, 1960.

Baker, Charles F. *A Dispensational Theology.* Grand Rapids: Grace Bible College Publications, 1980.

Barclay, William. *The Gospel of Matthew.* vol. 1. Philadelphia: The Westminster Press, 1958.

_____. *The Revelation of John.* Philadelphia: The Westminster Press, 1960.

Barnes, Albert. *Notes on the New Testament.* Grand Rapids: Baker Book House, 1949.

Bauer, Walter. *A Greek-English Lexicon of the New Testament and Other Early Christian Literature.* Translated by W. F. Arndt and F. W. Gingrich. Revised and augmented by F. W. Danker. Chicago: The University of Chicago Press, 1979.

Berkhof, Louis. *Systematic Theology.* Grand Rapids: William B. Eerdmans Publishing, 1961.

Brown, France, S. R. Driver, Charles A. Briggs. *A Hebrew and English Lexicon of the Old Testament.* Edited by William Gesenius. Oxford: The Clarendon Press, 1962.

Bruce, F. F. *The Book of Acts.* The New Testament Commentary on the New Testament. Grand Rapids: William B. Eerdmans Publishing Company, 1989.

_____. *The Epistle to the Hebrews.* The New Testament Commentary on the New Testament. Grand Rapids: William B. Eerdmans Publishing Company, 1985.

Calvin, John. *The Institutes of the Christian Religion.* Grand Rapids: Associated Publishers and Authors, n. d.

Chafer, Lewis Sperry. *Systematic Theology.* 8 vols. Dallas: Dallas Theological Seminary, 1948.

Cocoris, G. Michael. *Evangelism: A Biblical Approach.* Chicago: Moody Press, 1984.

Dana, H. E. and Julius R. Mantey. *A Manual Grammar of the Greek New Testament.* New York: The Macmillan Company, 1959.

Edersheim, Alfred. *In the Days of Christ: Sketches of Jewish Social Life.* New York: Revell, 1876.

Erickson, Millard J. *Christian Theology.* Grand Rapids: Baker Book House, 1990.

Evans, Williams. *The Great Doctrines of the Bible.* Chicago: Moody Press, 1949.

Geldenhuys, Norval. *Commentary on Luke.* New International Commentary on the New Testament. Grand Rapids: William B. Eerdmans Publishing Company, 1983.

Gill, John. *The Exposition of the New Testament.* London: George Keith, 1774.

Gloag, Paton J. *A Critical and Exegetical Commentary on the Acts of the Apostles.* Minneapolis: Klock and Klock Christian Publishers, 1979.

Godet, F. L. *Commentary on the Gospel of John.* 2 vols. Grand Rapids: Zondervan Publishing House, 1883.

_____. *Commentary on the Gospel of St. Luke.* 2 vols. Grand Rapids: Zondervan Publishing House, 1887.

Guthrie, Donald. *Hebrews.* Tyndale New Testament Commentary. Grand Rapids: William B. Eerdmans Publishing Company, 1986.

Hadjiantoniou, G. A. *The Postman of Patmos.* Grand Rapids: Zondervan Publishing House, 1961.

Hanson, Bradley C. *Introduction to Christian Theology.* Minneapolis: Fortress Press, 1997.

Hodges, Zane C. *Absolutely Free.* Grand Rapids: Zondervan Publishing House, 1989.

_____. "Hebrews" in *The Bible Knowledge Commentary.* Edited by John F. Walvoord and Roy B. Zuck. Wheaton, Illinois: Victor Books, 1983.

Ironside, Harry A. *Except Ye Repent.* New York: American Tract Society, 1937.

Kelly, J. N. D. *A Commentary on the Pastoral Epistles.* Grand Rapids: Baker Book House, 1986.

Kent, Jr., Homer A. *The Epistle to the Hebrews.* Grand Rapids: Baker Book House, 1974.

_____. *The Pastoral Epistles.* Chicago: Moody Press, 1966.

Kittel, Gerhard, Gerhard Friedrich, and Geoffrey W. Bromiley. *Theological Dictionary of the New Testament*. Translated by Geoffrey W. Bromiley. Index compiled by Ronald E. Pitkin. 10 vols. Grand Rapids: William B. Eerdmans Publishing Company, 1964-76.

Kruse, Colin. *2 Corinthians*. Tyndale New Testament Commentary. Grand Rapids: William B. Eerdmans Publishing Company, 1987.

Lane, William L. *Commentary on the Gospel of Mark*. New International Commentary on the New Testament. Grand Rapids: William B. Eerdmans Publishing Company, 1984.

Lang, G. H. *The Epistle to the Hebrews*. London: The Paternoster Press, 1951.

Liddell, H. G. and Robert Scott. *An Intermediate Greek-English Lexicon*. New York: Harper & Brothers Publishers, 1894.

Lenski, Richard C. H. *Interpretation of the Acts of the Apostles*. Minneapolis: Augsburg, 1961.

_____. *Interpretation of the St. Matthew*. Minneapolis: Augsburg, 1961.

_____. *Interpretation of Hebrews*. Minneapolis: Augsburg, 1961.

_____. *Interpretation of the Luke's Gospel*. Minneapolis: Augsburg, 1961.

Marshall, I. Howard. *Acts*. Tyndale New Testament Commentary. Grand Rapids: William B. Eerdmans Publishing Company, 1986.

Mantey, Julius R. "Repentance and Conversion" in *Basic Christian Doctrine*. Edited by Carl F. H. Henry. New York: Holt Rinehart and Winston, 1962.

M'Neile, Alan Hugh. *The Gospel According to St. Matthew*. London: Macmillan and Company, 1961.

Morris, Leon. *The Gospel According to St. Luke*. Tyndale New Testament Commentary. Grand Rapids: William B. Eerdmans Publishing Company, 1986.

Moulton, James Hope and George Milligan. *The Vocabulary of the Greek Testament*. Grand Rapids: William B. Eerdmans Publishing Company, 1972.

Mounce, Robert H. *The Book of Revelation*. Grand Rapids: William B. Eerdmans Publishing Company, 1977.

Newell, William R. *Hebrews Verse by Verse*. Chicago: Moody Press, 1947.

Robertson, A. T. *Word Pictures in the New Testament*. Nashville: Broadman, 1932.

Ryrie, Charles C. *Basic Theology*. Wheaton, Illinois: Victor Books, 1986.

_____. *A Survey of Bible Doctrine*. Chicago: Moody Press, 1972.

_____. *So Great Salvation*. Wheaton, Illinois: Victor Books, 1989.

Plummer, Alfred. *The Gospel According to St. Luke*. International Critical Commentary. New York: Charles Scribner's Sons, 1903.

Simpson, E. K. *The Pastoral Epistles*. London: Tyndale Press,1954.

Smith, J. B. *A Revelation of Jesus Christ*. Scottdale, PA: Herald Press, 1961.

Strong, A. H. *Systemic Theology*. Philadelphia: Judson Press, 1907.

Tasker, R. V. G. *2 Corinthians*. Tyndale New Testament Commentary. Grand Rapids: William B. Eerdmans Publishing Company, 1983.

Torrey, R. A. *What the Bible Teaches*. New York: Revell, 1898.

Toussaint, Stanley D. "Acts." In *The Bible Knowledge Commentary*. Edited by John F. Walvoord and Roy B. Zuck. Wheaton, IL: Victor Books, 1983.

Trench, Richard Chenevix. *Synonyms of the New Testament*. Grand Rapids: William B. Eerdmans Publishing Company, 1963.

Walvoord, John F. *The Revelation of Jesus Christ*. Chicago: Moody Press, 1966.

Westcott, B. F. *The Epistle to the Hebrews*. Grand Rapids: William B. Eerdmans Publishing Company, 1965.

_____. *The Gospel According to John*. London: James Clarke, 1958.

Wilkin, Robert N. "Does Your Mind Need Changing? Repentance Reconsidered." *Journal of the Grace Evangelical Society* 11 (Spring 1998).

_____. "Repentance as a Condition for Salvation in the New Testament." Th.D. dissertation, Dallas Theological Seminary, 1985.

_____. "The Doctrine of Repentance in Church History." *Journal of the Grace Evangelical Society* 1 (Autumn 1988).

_____. "The Doctrine of Repentance in the Old Testament." *Journal of the Grace Evangelical Society* 2 (Spring 1989).

_____. "The Doctrine of Repentance: Lexical Considerations." *Journal of the Grace Evangelical Society* 2 (Autumn 1989).

_____. "New Testament Repentance: Repentance in the Gospels and Acts." *Journal of the Grace Evangelical Society* 3 (Spring 1990).

_____. "The Doctrine of Repentance in the Epistles and Revelation." *Journal of the Grace Evangelical Society* 3 (Autumn 1990).

_____. "Preaching and Teaching about Repentance." *Journal of the Grace Evangelical Society* 4 (Spring 1991).

Würthwein, E. "*metanoeō, metanoia*." In *Theological Dictionary of the New Testament*. Edited by Gerhard Kittel, Gerhard Friedrich, and Geoffrey W. Bromiley. Translated by Geoffrey W. Bromiley. Index compiled by Ronald E. Pitkin. 10 vols. Grand Rapids: William B. Eerdmans Publishing Company, 1964-76. 4:975-1009.

Scripture Index

CPSIA information can be obtained at www.ICGtesting.com
Printed in the USA
BVOW05s0242190314

348112BV00010B/309/P